T0198591

From
OUR HOME
to
OUR HEROES

From
OUR HOME
to
OUR HEROES

The Story of Operation Troop Support

DICK MOODY

FROM OUR HOME TO OUR HEROES
THE STORY OF OPERATION TROOP SUPPORT

iUniverse books may be ordered through booksellers or by contacting:

iUniverse
1663 Liberty Drive
Bloomington, IN 47403
www.iuniverse.com
844-349-9409

Because of the dynamic nature of the Internet, any web addresses or links contained in this book may have changed since publication and may no longer be valid. The views expressed in this work are solely those of the author and do not necessarily reflect the views of the publisher, and the publisher hereby disclaims any responsibility for them.

Any people depicted in stock imagery provided by Getty Images are models, and such images are being used for illustrative purposes only.
Certain stock imagery © Getty Images.

ISBN: 978-1-6632-4429-1 (sc)
ISBN: 978-1-6632-4428-4 (e)

Library of Congress Control Number: 2023900672

Print information available on the last page.

iUniverse rev. date: 02/03/2023

This book has a three-part dedication:

First, to my wife, Christine, who has worked tirelessly in our home for twenty years to ensure that the American soldier is well cared for

Second, to the families impacted by the horrendous events of September 11, 2001, from which Operation Troop Support was born

Third, to the American soldier, who has put his or her life on the line to protect the American way of life

C O N T E N T S

FOREWORD

It was a week after my retired military husband's death in 2004. I was trying to adjust my life and was catching up on local newspapers when I noted an article about a new program being initiated, focusing on military service members. As wife and daughter of career US Army men, I was always interested in programs related to them, so I read on. The organizers were asking veterans, military spouses, and any interested local citizens to come to a meeting in nearby Danvers, Massachusetts, to find out more. Called "Operation Troop Support," the program was unfamiliar to me, and I admit I was somewhat suspicious of it, so I decided to attend and check it out.

That evening, I joined a mixed group of strangers at a VFW site, where we were warmly welcomed by the leader. He identified himself as Dick Moody, a retired air force officer. He said he was hoping to recruit volunteers from the community who could help acquire, pack up, and mail items that military personnel serving overseas in challenging situations, including war zones, had said they had missed since leaving the States. There were no funds for purchasing items or even for mailing donated items to the troops, so here was another need to be addressed.

Colonel Moody then asked us who we were and what had brought us to this meeting. Going around the room, we heard from retired veterans, spouses from military members already abroad, and local citizens with friends in service. Then we noticed an elder pair with a young couple at their side. The senior said, "This is my son and the wife he just married today. They had seen your meeting written up and felt they had better attend because my son is being deployed to Iraq this week. We thought it might be important to find out what you are doing for the troops he'll be joining." At that point, much of the audience began wiping away tears. Now we knew why we were there.

Since that day, nearly twenty years ago, I have come to appreciate the founder of Operation Troop Support, Dick Moody, and his devoted wife and life partner, Christine, for being true patriots with a mission that has become more meaningful every year. They have never flagged in their commitment, and their uplifting example in giving service has been contagious to so many others. Because it has been supported by increasing numbers of volunteers and donors over the years who have come to understand how they can make a positive difference, Operation Troop Support has always delivered as pledged.

Assembling and delivering multiple thousands of welcome gifts to our service personnel serving in harm's way has been a mission that only a leader dedicated to a genuinely worthy cause could have accomplished. The countless heartfelt thank-you notes from soldier recipients give full evidence that the task was worth the effort. The Operation Troop Support history, still continuing, is indeed worthy of being told. There are lessons for our world today and going forward that Dick and Christine Moody are more than capable of inspiring. I am thankful that they have chosen to share their story with us.

—Joanne Holbrook Patton
Wife of Major General George Patton

INTRODUCTION

March 19, 2003, forever will be etched in our minds as the day the United States invaded Iraq. I remember the cold, cloudy day in Boston; the only good thing about the New England winter was that the days were getting longer, teasing everyone that spring was just around the corner.

March 19, 2003, will also be remembered for another reason. The day was quieting down, and I was about to turn on the TV for the beginning of our nightly ritual, when, at 7:30, the telephone rang. It was our daughter Christina-Marie, whom we call Tina. She was calling from Germany, where she was a combat medic in the Intensive Care Unit of Landstuhl Regional Medical Center at Ramstein Air Force Base. My wife joined us on the call, and after a few pleasantries, Tina told us why she was calling. It seems that her patients, destined to travel home to Walter Reed army hospital for recovery, had been given all the magazines available in the Medical Center to take with them, leaving her in-house wounded soldiers with few, if any, items to divert their minds from the pain of recovery. If possible, could we send her some books, magazines, or games to pass on to the patients? Christine said sure, and at that moment, the mission of Operation Troop Support was born.

As an appropriate way to start this story, let me tell you a little about my wife of fifty-two years, Christine, and me. Following my graduation from college, I signed up for the United States Air Force, where I was sent to Officer Training School (OTS) at Lackland Air Force Base in Texas. The plans my soon-to-be-wife Christine and I had agreed on included an OTS graduation on April 2, 1970, our wedding two days later on April 4, and then a very quick honeymoon before driving to my pilot training base in Georgia, aptly named Moody Air Force Base, in the town of Valdosta, no later than April 11.

On my last training day in Texas, I ran into a problem when fighting the simulated enemy in the field, and I had to call Christine from the hospital to tell her I had been bitten by a rattlesnake, to which she promptly accused me of not wanting to come home and marry her. She finally realized I was serious, and fortunately, I was still able to come home on schedule, since the bite had not broken through my combat boot. Once I arrived home, the wedding went off without a hitch. After fifty-two years of a wonderful marriage, however, I think I've finally convinced her that the snake bite really did happen, and it was not an excuse to break off the big day.

My first assignment was Syracuse, New York, at the Twenty-First Air Division of the North American Aerospace Defense Command (NORAD), controlling fighter aircraft for one year, before leaving for Southeast Asia. Upon my return in 1973, I was cycled through a variety of assignments that included stateside tours at Syracuse; McChord AFB in Washington State; Tyndall AFB in Florida; Fort Lee army post, Virginia; Maxwell AFB in Montgomery, Alabama; Canadian Forces Defense Headquarters at North Bay, Ontario; Hofn NATO Base, Iceland; Miyako Jima, Okinawa; Hickam AFB in Hawaii; and Hanscom AFB in Massachusetts.

In 1993, I retired from the US Air Force after twenty-three years, and my civilian job gave me similar opportunities to experience family separations. I traveled to Saudi Arabia, Kuwait, Mozambique, South Africa, Israel, the West Bank, and the Gaza Strip, as well as Korea (twice), Switzerland, England, Taiwan, and Mexico. With this type of travel experience, it was easy to see how fortunate we were to live in America and enjoy the freedoms that we do today.

These assignments took me all over the world, and while I was away, Christine served our country as well. Everything we owned was crammed into our Dodge sedan as we drove 1,200 miles to Georgia to start our lives together in 1970. In the years following our first assignment, she pursued her Air Force career through volunteer positions at the various bases and had our first child, David, while I was serving during Vietnam. I finally got to meet him when he was two months old. Dave got to see the entire country with us as a young son, and as he grew, his life took many turns that made us so proud of him. He was a star athlete as the captain of the high school football team. After studying criminal justice at Northeastern University, Dave went on to become a top manager for a security company and took charge of security oversight for several shopping malls, high-rise condos, and Boston Garden, the home of the Celtics and the Bruins.

As the years went on, we had three more wonderful children. Our second son, Scott, was born at an army hospital in Washington State while we were stationed at McChord AFB at the Twenty-Fifth Air Division of NORAD. Years later, after graduating from high school, where he excelled in sports and theater arts, he entered the US Air Force and was trained as a member of the Air Police, both in the States and overseas during the Iraq/Afghanistan conflict. After twenty-two years of active duty, he retired as a senior master sergeant. Our first daughter, Amy Lynn, was born with dual citizenship while we were stationed in North Bay, Ontario, Canada. In high school, Amy was the drum major of the high school marching band, then entered college, where she received her degree and went on to become a human resources executive at a variety of companies. Our second daughter, Tina-Marie, came when we returned to Hanscom AFB in Massachusetts. Tina was the captain of the color guard in high school and excelled in the theater arts programs. Following graduation, she enlisted in the US Air Force and embarked on a medical career. Following her assignment in Iraq, she was awarded her college degree in nursing and today is a registered nurse in the Veterans Administration hospital in Bedford, Massachusetts.

Over the next few years, we spent a lot of time traveling across the country from the Pacific Northwest to the Deep South, up both coasts, down to Mexico, through the Canadian Rockies to the Canadian Forces Defense Headquarters in North Bay, Ontario, back to Montgomery, Alabama, and up to New England. Through it all, Christine managed to balance the role of military wife, loving mother, and community volunteer. She took courses at Middlesex Community College in Massachusetts, and while we were stationed in Canada, she taught at Canadore College and started her own business as a professional cake decorator. When Dave became preschool age and there was no nursery school available, Christine obtained approval from the Canadian Ministry of Education and started a nursery school in town, complete with finding a location, hiring a teacher, recruiting several families, and working out a top-notch curriculum. Once we returned to the States, she became very active in the American Legion and VFW auxiliaries.

The loneliness that a deployed soldier and his or her family feels is brutal, and it is compounded by poor living conditions, a strange country, a different language, and customs that are foreign. The experiences we shared during our twenty-three years in the service were tough, with our nineteen different moves, two remote tours, and no care packages received during the Vietnam War. On March 19, 2003, some thirty years after that conflict ended, Christine and I decided that now would be a good time to give back to our country, and sending care packages would be a great way to do it.

At the time, we didn't know it, but on that night, we began a journey that would change our lives. This simple phone call was about to impact the lives of thousands of young men and women across America, and our lives would be changed in a way that cannot be adequately described in the pages of a small book.

Come with us as we relate some of our most precious memories that we came to hold so dear as we took Operation Troop Support (OTS) on a fascinating journey that reached many, many American lives.

As you will see in the following pages, Operation Troop Support has been able to care for the deployed soldiers on the battlefield and in the combat support hospitals as well as their families on the home front. We have spoken to all kinds of organizations and groups about what the troops want, met with dignitaries regarding the needs of the soldiers, traveled to Iraq to meet with the wounded troops, and been there to say goodbye to the servicemen and servicewomen and rushed to welcome them home. We have received the George Washington Medal of Freedom award twice, the national Very Important Patriot Award, the Citizen of the Year, a place on the Federal Register, and many local and state awards. How did we do all of this? The answer lies in one easy response: the good people who have helped us along the way.

Christine and I have been blessed with so many wonderful, caring people who have given to our country through our group—their time, items, or money to help our deployed soldiers and their loved ones at home. It would be impossible to list everyone who has helped us over the years, but we think every day of those good people who took the extra step above and beyond, and we hold a special place in our hearts for each one of them.

Setting The Course

Working with the Post Office

When we hung up the phone from talking to Tina on March 19, 2003, Christine and I started collecting all the magazines, toiletries, and other miscellaneous items we could find and then looked for a box to ship them in. As the weeks went on, with the help of son Dave and our daughter-in-law Heidi, we packed care packages and sent them to Tina. We also reached out to our son Scott, a member of an Air Force Security Police squadron at the time, who also was deployed overseas. We received voluntary assistance from several friends, including Charlene Potter, who was the first person outside the family to make a donation.

The Danvers postmaster was very personable, but he informed me that any care package we brought in would have to be treated in the same as any other box, meaning that we needed to bring the package into the lobby and wait in line for a counter representative to become available. Ordinarily, this would seem a logical requirement, but within a few weeks, I would go to the post office with twenty-five to thirty boxes at a time, and I would have to find a parking space close to the steps leading to the front door. Once parked, I would make repeated trips up the steps and into the lobby, where I was told to stack the packages beside me in line and walk with them up to the counter.

Eventually, the post office staff allowed me to bring the boxes into the lobby and stack them up by the counter, making it easier for me to stand in line and keep my eye on them as I approached the postal employees. Of course, it must have been a bit unnerving for the other people standing in the postal line to see me walking in with box after box, cutting to the front of the line, and dropping my packages directly in front of the window.

The post office employees were helpful to me, however, and provided a list of APO and FPO codes for us to use as a reference. These codes were essentially the ZIP codes for the overseas troops. APO stood for Army/Air Force Post Office, and FPO stood for Fleet Post Office. The boxes going to APOs were sent out of a port in New York and would get to their destination in a little over a week, but the FPOs, the Fleet Post Office, were shipped out of San Diego, California, and it took almost two weeks to get to the troops at those FPO locations.

As 2003 turned into 2004, more friends and acquaintances came out to join us. Carol Slavin, whose son TJ was in Iraq, was quick to respond. The Brennans' son Derek was deployed, so they were a huge help, as were Tom and MaryLee Angers, whose son was down range as well. Bob and Nan Blanchette came out, as did Pat Johnson, a Peabody resident, who became a very dear friend over the years. After finding out that we were sending care packages to the troops, other people began to pose questions and asked if they could help us out. People began dropping off bags or boxes of items, including books and magazines, toiletries, food snacks, playing cards, and socks. Because so many people were calling and asking for suggestions on what to send, we developed a website and included a listing of potential donations. Separate lists showed items needed in the desert, as well as the hospitals, including food, toiletries, and other miscellaneous articles.

One day, I received an invitation to attend the change-of-command ceremony to welcome the new postmaster of Danvers, Ms. Brenda

Martin. Brenda became a good friend and was very helpful to us. She introduced us to the flat-rate boxes, which the post office would supply at no cost to us. She advised us to order these online, as they were shipped out daily and were more apt to have a larger supply than the local post office might have. In addition, she helped us with the paperwork that was required on our boxes and instructed us on how to fill out the multiple-copy custom form. I would fill out the appropriate information, describe the contents of the package, and then pay the required postage. The biggest piece of good news we received from Brenda was that whenever we had packages, we could drive to the back of the post office and unload our boxes onto the loading dock, where the postal employees would bring them inside to attach the mailing labels.

I was a member of VFW Post 2359 of Danvers, and we met the fourth Tuesday of the month at the VFW Hall, directly across the street from the post office. We had some great patriots in our organization. My friends in the post were guys like Roland Kelly, a World War II pilot, who owned a couple of automobile dealerships in town; Eddie Poitras, an army private who we called "Frenchy" because of his European heritage and background from the French neighborhood of Salem, where he grew up; and Dick Lilja, a navy corpsman who wore his love of the navy on his arm, next to the love of his life, Ruth, a staunch marine who kept the old sea salt in line. These guys, along with the rest of the post, liked what our group of volunteers was doing to help the deployed troops and decided to help us out.

VFW Members helping with OTS donations

We began a two-way street, with our group becoming the community service arm of the Danvers VFW, which led to the National VFW awarding our post the National Community Service Award for three of the next four years. In return, the post gave us postage funds to mail the care packages overseas.

VFW members loading the truck on mailing day

As the weeks went on, Christine and I realized we needed to have a name associated with our care-package program, so we had a meeting with the volunteers. As we discussed the issue at hand, Christine recommended that we call ourselves Operation Troop Support. It was an excellent suggestion that everyone approved of, but when we went to register this name with the Commonwealth of Massachusetts, we found that the name had already been taken by another group. So, after some discussion, we became Troop Support USA, and the name was born. Troop Support USA was shown in the papers, on flyers, on bumper stickers, and on calling cards. Troop Support USA quickly became recognized in Danvers, as the newspaper interviewed us due to the public's interest in the ongoing war, and the Danvers VFW became a popular organization, with a community service program that was very well received. When we found out that the name Operation Troop Support had become available, we jumped at the chance to switch to that name, and it has been OTS ever since. One of our volunteers Dave Brennan came up with the slogan, "Help Us Help Them," which was very descriptive of where our hearts were. The slogan has been imprinted on our logo since that day.

For the next several months, the weeks passed with daily packing and trips to the Danvers Post Office. The VFW post allowed us to do some packing at the VFW Hall, and then some of the VFW members helped bring the sealed boxes to the post office for shipment overseas. People in the town were very eager to help bring the boxes to the post office, and many of the neighbors dropped by our home several times during the week to pick up the care packages and bring them downtown. A constant helper was Bud Dugas, who drove a small Volkswagen. Ordinarily, Bud was able to transfer all of our packages on any given day, but one day, we had a few too many. He filled his entire car but had one left. Not to be defeated, Bud rolled down his window in freezing weather and grabbed the last box. The people of Danvers saw him rolling down Trinity Street with his arm holding the package out the window. Our volunteers went the extra mile for us, even in a VW Bug.

Because we were running everything out of our home and the VFW, we reported our care-package activity to Headquarters VFW in Kansas City, and one day, I received a call from HQ, wanting to interview us on our program. A very nice young lady asked a lot of questions regarding how we collected the items, how we paid for the postage, and where the packages went when they left Danvers. A few weeks later, an excellent article appeared in the National VFW newsletter, explaining how the small town of Danvers, Massachusetts, was contributing to the war effort and helping the troops. This exposure fueled the patriotic fire that so many Americans were looking for, and, as a result, the phone calls multiplied, the mail expanded, and the word of mouth spread, resulting in a huge increase in interest from people wanting to help the American soldier.

The OTS Public Pack

The time finally came when the amount of daily donations became much more than our few volunteers could handle, so we made plans to open up a packing event to the public. Many people came forward, wanting to be a part of this, and we welcomed all who called.

As it was our initial packing event, Christine and I began to think of the things that we needed to cover. The first thing that came to mind was to determine how many items were needed to keep a lot of people busy on a Saturday. In retrospect, this is where we underestimated the enthusiasm and the speed of the American people. We figured we would be in the hall most of the day. Instead, just two hours after we started, voices began to say, "Are there any more items?" Well now, I can tell you that the next pack would be different.

I'm getting ahead of myself. We put the word out that the pack was coming, and we adjusted our website to show specific items that were popular at the different months of the year. This helped people decide what to donate to us for the pack. We began getting wonderful donations, and in our minds, this was proof that the public cared and wanted to play a part in sending packages to the troops. The one challenge we tended to overlook was the question of where to store the items as we prepared for the event. When people found out we were scheduling a pack, they would drop off bags or boxes of donated items. This, in turn, created a need for space in our home to store the goods so we could screen them and place them into the containers that would be taken to the event. By the day of the pack, our living room, dining room, kitchen, and hallways were loaded with items. We committed quite a bit of time to checking each item to make sure everything we had was allowable and appropriate. Volunteers checked donated food products to ensure they were not stale dated, and they removed any glass containers or aerosol cans. We could not ship these due to the chance of a pressure buildup that would cause breakage or explosion en route. Any such items were put aside to hand carry to the Veterans Administration hospital.

Christine was very cognizant of the care we had to provide to make sure the packages made it to their destination intact. We decided that all items that could spill or ruin the other items were to be put into Ziploc bags for protection. While this required a lot of extra work, here is where the volunteers were a tremendous help to us. We needed a huge amount of gallon-, quart-, sandwich-, and snack-size Ziploc bags for use in preparing the products. We kept food and nonfood items separated into different containers because food items picked up the scent of soap or other toiletry products—considering the long trip these products would take, we did not want the potato chips tasting like Irish Spring soap.

Once the items were sorted and bagged, we were ready to have the public come and pack the care packages. Some of our volunteers came by the house early on the day of the pack and helped us load the containers of items into vehicles for transport to the VFW. Vans or pickup trucks could only handle so much, but the good people of Bourbon Street Storage in Peabody offered one of their box trucks to us, and that was a lifesaver. The truck was filled, and we were on our way to the VFW in downtown Danvers Square.

Our volunteers had tape guns ready, pencils in hand for the custom forms, and two-wheelers poised to take the filled boxes across the street to the post office. Nine o'clock came, and the doors were unlocked. Do you remember the scene in the Jimmy Stewart movie *It's a Wonderful Life*, when the bank was out of money, and all the depositors wanted to break down the doors to get what little money was left? When we unlocked the VFW doors that morning, all I could think of was Jimmy Stewart. Hundreds of people, eager to make a care package for a soldier, came rushing through that door, nearly trampling each other in an attempt to get to a table and do something good. We had young folks, old folks, college students, scouts, Little Leaguers, and so many more that we lost count.

We had done a good job with the room setup. The tables were placed together in long rows to form a production line appearance. One of our volunteers taped empty boxes together at one end of the tables. Each member of the public would take one of these empty boxes and walk along the table, take an item out of the containers on the table, and put it into the empty box. Once their boxes were full, they would put them on a designated table in another part of the room. Here, the boxes would be examined by a couple of our volunteers to ensure they were filled to the top. If a box was taped up with space in it, it was more apt to get crushed in transit or ripped apart. It was in this area that any inserts would be added to the care package—inserts that told the soldier who the sponsors of the items were and also a Care Package Request (CPR) form to be used by someone other than our point of contact, who might want to get future packages. We included the form in a blank envelope, along with a pen to fill it out and return it to us. This mechanism put us in touch with hundreds of soldiers, sailors, airmen, marines, guardsmen and guardswomen, and even reservists deployed to the region. The completed boxes were then taped up and put on the cart to bring to the truck or the post office.

By the end of the day, we had packed over two hundred care packages. Everything was gone, and the VFW was back to normal. We were ecstatic at the number of people who had showed up; everyone who had taken part was thrilled to be a part of something good. The post office was in shock at the amount of work looking back at them. The pack was a great event to show people how we prepared items for the soldiers. The families took a great deal of pride in packing their own boxes, and the friendships made on that day stayed with us for years. Christine and I went home to our empty house and decided to have a drink and relax. It was a good day for the troops.

Items to be packed

Public packing the boxes

Bringing The Families Aboard

Family Support Group (FSG)

By the spring of 2004, the Iraq War was on everyone's mind, and we began to notice an interesting change taking place. Many of the people who contacted us would ask us about the items needed by the soldiers, but there seemed to be a high degree of tension in their voices. For many of the families, this separation was the first time their loved one had been away from home, and coping with this separation was almost too much to bear, especially when the daily television, radio, and newspaper reports were filled with gruesome details and horrifying statistics. Some of the mothers broke down on the phone, and some of the spouses became nearly hysterical as we tried to quiet them down. We sympathized with these families because we could feel their pain. Christine and I had gone through twenty-three years of military service, with two remote tours, one during Vietnam, and we knew that a separation of a family member is very difficult to take.

Given the clear need for some type of help, we decided to host a Family Support Group (FSG) to give these family members some support to get through the separation. We set to work on plans to develop a monthly FSG meeting, complete with professional speakers and counselors to help guide the families along their way.

Now, from the outset, we acknowledged that neither of us was a trained therapist or counselor, but we had been through the dreary days and sleepless nights and could lend a hand to the families while helping out their loved ones. We were blessed by having Hanscom Air Force Base, with its trained personnel, less than one hour away, along with the Veterans Administration facilities within a similar distance from our community. With this team of specialists so close to our town, we decided to start the FSG at the VFW hall in the summer of 2004. We printed up some flyers with our name, along with the nature and place of the meeting, and put them up around town. In addition, we placed an ad in the local papers, and spread the word to anyone we thought would be interested. The third Thursday evening of the month at seven o'clock was set aside for our meetings, and although we did not have any idea who might show up, we put together a program to introduce the public to the Operation Troop Support Family Support Group.

From our own experience and with help from different military family support organizations, we developed an agenda that would introduce newcomers into the group, give out pertinent information that would be of interest to everyone, bring in guest speakers or specialists, and schedule events that would bring the families together. Our first FSG meeting was scheduled for July 15, 2004. We had no idea if anyone would show up, but we had our agenda and hoped that some family members who we had talked to during the past few months would come. No guest speaker was scheduled, as we thought the first meeting would be limited to introductions and general questions.

The night of the fifteenth arrived, and at seven o'clock, a few people began to wander into the hall. I was the designated emcee, and I waited for a few minutes to make sure everyone had a chance to get a cup of coffee and a muffin, which we had put out on the table. After explaining why the meeting had been called, Christine and I went around the room to the thirteen people who had come. Everyone gave their names and the names of their deployed loved ones. It was the wedding day of one of the couples, but since he was about to deploy later that night, they wanted to set up his new wife with a group to help her cope with his absence.

Everyone had a story, and all of the attendees seemed very sincere in their fears and apprehension. They thanked us for putting this meeting together because it gave them the opportunity to share their emotions with others who were going through the same ordeal. After nearly everyone had spoken, there was one person left in the back corner of the room who had not yet introduced herself to the group. She very graciously stood and stated that although she did not have a family member currently overseas in Iraq, she had been a military spouse for thirty years and a military widow of two weeks. Her name was Mrs. Joanne Patton, whose husband, Major General George Patton, had passed away on June 27, just two weeks earlier.

Christine and I were amazed that Joanne had decided to come to our meeting, but in the years that followed, she became a trusted and dear friend, an invaluable asset to OTS, and an amazing mentor who has guided us through many difficult circumstances over the years.

We left that first meeting on July 15 excited that we might be able to make a difference with some of the families, and we set to work doing some research into which tools were available for us to recommend to the community. After that night, we continued to send out weekly packages to the battlefield and hospitals, but we also concentrated our efforts on the Family Support Group. We reviewed books that had been written on deployment and got copies of these books for the people to read. We gathered telephone numbers and pamphlets and brochures from organizations that focused their attention on preparing for, coping with, and dealing with the aftermath of a military separation. We suffered through the challenge of raising postage funds, but we believed the families needed our help as much as the soldier who was tens of thousands of miles away.

Families listening to a guest speaker

The Family Support Group meetings had introduced many family members, relatives, or friends to trained professionals and had given them an opportunity to talk about the fears and concerns that consumed them while waiting for their loved ones to return from Iraq, Afghanistan, Kuwait, or other faraway places.

As part of our Family Support Group, we brought in stress counselors, lawyers, and employment experts to discuss ways to help the returning troops and their families. Veterans Administration specialists were brought in to answer questions on benefits, disability compensation, housing, loans, taxes, and a host of other matters, such as "Coping with the Stress of Separation," "Traumatic Brain Injury (TBI)," "Military to Civilian Transition Assistance," "Signs of Suicide," and "Bills before Congress for Soldiers' Rights."

So many people in town wanted to get involved. The Family Support Group seemed to be a fruitful addition to the mission, and we received good turnouts on the nights that returning soldiers paid us a visit. The accounts from the men and women who had served in country were invaluable and generated a lot of questions. We even brought in the owner of a therapeutic horse farm and service-dog trainers to brief on these specialty services.

OTS was becoming a household name, but we thought there could be other things we might do to alleviate the fear associated with a deployment.

Holiday Packages

As the holiday season approached, Christine suggested that we send an individually wrapped Christmas gift to every soldier with whom we communicated. We thought it would be a good idea to give everyone a gift, not just our point of contact. A "Christmas wrap," in which the public would participate, was planned, but we were not sure how much room we needed to do this. I decided to try the VFW again, in spite of the organized chaos the first packing event had caused. The maximum number of people for the VFW was eighty on each of the two floors, so we thought that would be enough room.

I sent out a letter or email to each of those soldiers who had contacted us over the year. In this letter, I asked them to let me know, if it did not infringe on any security issue, how many men and women were in their respective units. The answers started coming back: seventeen soldiers, twenty-two, nineteen, twenty-six, etc. We were feeling pretty good that we were getting a handle on this when a young marine wrote to us and told us he had 3,300 men in his group. Yikes! Now what would we do? Time to regroup or press ahead? As usual, we decided to press ahead and see what happened.

With the 3,300 gifts added to the others, we needed to come up with nearly four thousand within the next few weeks to send. We put an ad in the local paper with a list of five new items to serve as gift ideas. The paper came out on Thursday, and by the following Monday, we had nearly ten thousand new gifts at the house. This was far beyond our expectations, but we were thrilled at the outpouring of help that came in. Now we hoped that we would get the appropriate turnout to take care of the thousands of presents slated to go to the soldiers.

Well, we were not disappointed. The hall was packed, and we had men, women, boys, girls, old people, young people, Danvers residents, people from other communities, and some from other states. A few wrinkles developed, such as running out of tape or holiday tags, but overall, it went very well. One great thing I noticed, which will stay with me forever, were the bikers. Everyone knows when the bikers come to town by the roar of the motorcycles, like trumpets announcing the arrival of the king.

Everyone turned and watched as the pack sat on their prized possessions for a few minutes after coming to a stop. Engines were still running, just for the effect, and then they dismounted, pretty much all at the same time. Here's where it gets good: they spent a few minutes making sure everything was in order—the vests were neat, the beards were in good shape, the helmets were slowly coming off—and then they started the slow saunter into the building, as if waiting to be announced to the audience. Oh, I was impressed beyond words! I decided to go up to them and give them a friendly welcome. Hey, you know what? These guys and gals were pretty good-natured. Now the kicker: a few minutes later, they were down on the floor, wrapping gifts next to a troop of Girl Scouts, talking to them about their kids, asking about the scouting program, and just being great Americans.

People, listen to me—you will not find more patriotic Americans than the bikers. I have spent time with them, gone on rides with them, and had meals with them, and they are true Americans, waving the flag whenever possible. I am proud to know them.

Within the hour, four thousand gifts were wrapped and seven thousand cards were filled out, and the Danvers Post Office didn't know what hit them! I was so proud of our town for their support of the American soldier.

The post office sent all the boxes out, and I wrote to our marine who had asked for the 3,300 gifts. I advised him that 3,300 gifts took up a lot of space in the boxes. Would he be able to deal with them while he was in Iraq, fighting the bad guy? He wrote back and told me not to worry because he had set up a distribution plan. He made it sound like we were a large production plant, but I told him to press on.

Everyone is so happy to be wrapping a gift for a soldier

Feedback from the Battlefield

It was about a week after Christmas that when our marine contacted me, thanked me for the gifts, and told me he would be transferring back to Camp Lejeune, North Carolina, so he didn't need any more packages. I acknowledged him and told him to look us up if he was ever in the Boston area because I wanted to meet the soldier who passed out over three thousand gifts on the battlefield at Christmas.

Several months later, I received a telephone call at 7:00 p.m. The voice on the other end said, "Good evening, Lieutenant Colonel Moody. You may not remember me, but I'm the gunney sergeant you sent a bunch of gifts to last Christmas."

I started to laugh and answered, "I just don't go around sending 3,300 wrapped Christmas gifts to just anyone. You bet I remember you!"

The gunney asked if we were still having our FSG meetings on the third Thursday of the month because, if so, he and his wife and little boy would like to drive up to thank us in person. I was delighted and gave him directions to come to our meeting in a couple of days.

Then I called everyone I knew to tell them to come out for a great evening. Two days later, on Thursday evening at seven o'clock, true to his word, the gunney came into the VFW hall amid a loud explosion of applause. He proceeded to tell us how he had distributed the gifts under such challenging conditions.

This is a heartwarming story. He told us that two thousand of the gifts went by Apache or Blackhawk helicopters to some of the men assigned to the FOBs (forward operating bases), and he sent them out on December 23, but the rest he would deliver himself. He had an old Toyota box truck, and his maintenance team had welded two bull horn speakers to the top of the cab. Then they wired the speakers to a cassette player in the cab. The cassette he had chosen had lively Christmas tunes, such as "Jingle Bells," "It's Beginning to Look a Lot Like Christmas," "Deck the Halls," and so on. He told us that when he cranked up the volume, you could hear the music at least a half mile away.

To assist him on his mission, he had selected a corporal, who did not want to go, for obvious reasons. Then at one minute past midnight on Christmas morning, he came out of his barracks, fully clothed as Santa Claus, dressed from head to toe as the jolly old elf in the suit that his wife had sent from home. He got into the cab of the truck and spoke into the radio. He said, "Don't shoot me; I'm coming through." For the next six hours, he drove through the streets of the countryside, music blaring, going from outpost to outpost, handing out gifts from a carefully predetermined route.

At this point, someone asked him if he had been scared.

"Scared? You bet I was scared. Picture this: you are a lone sentry standing guard in the middle of the night, with the bad guys all around you. Suddenly, a box truck pulls up and stops about fifty feet away. The door opens up, and Santa Claus gets out and walks toward you, holding a box. Was I scared? What do you think? The thing is that once they found it was a gift from a person from the homeland, most of them would break down and weep. Someone back home remembered them."

He gave all the gifts away that night and made it back to the base by 6:00 a.m. He told us that when he got out of the truck, he looked up and said, "Thank you, God, for allowing me to give our soldiers a gift to open on Christmas morning before breakfast, just like home." When he said those words, there wasn't a dry eye in our room.

As the years went on, we brought our Christmas wraps to other locations. We usually tried to accommodate organizations when they called, and we would put boxes of items together to bring to that location. Examples of some of our wraps were the Reading Senior Center, Peabody Senior Center, Brooksby Village Senior Living Community, Revere Senior Center, Salem State University, Endicott College, Colby College, Malden Catholic High School, and St. John's Prep.

OTS would prepare the items to be shipped and load the boxes of these items into a truck, along with the packing supplies (Christmas paper, tape, pens, and tags). When we would get to the destination, a few volunteers would unload the cargo and bring it into the area to wrap, and then we would instruct the patrons how to do the work. Once the gifts had been wrapped, they would be loaded into the boxes, then onto the truck, and finally taken to the post office, where they would be processed for shipment.

Our Christmas wraps have been very successful, and that was due in large part to two of our most active volunteers, Steve and Ellen Godzik. I have known Steve nearly all my life, and I was thrilled when he volunteered to help us out on the OTS mission. Whenever Christine and I had a thought on how to draw public attention to our program, Steve would come up with ideas or designs to advance the cause. For example, he drew up the design for our tenth and fifteenth OTS anniversary pins, which we would be distributing on the appropriate anniversary dates.

He and his wife, Ellen, discussed the concept of a Christmas wrap with us, and we thought that a gift with five or six items wrapped up would be a nice package for the soldier to receive. Examples of the items that would make up the individual gift would be a pair of socks, a small toiletry kit, a deck of playing cards, a puzzle book or crossword puzzle book, and a candy of some sort. These items would be contained in a larger bag and then wrapped in Christmas paper. Some of the gifts would be for men, while others would be tailored to the female soldiers. As the gifts were put together, they would be placed in a large Ziploc bag and a "male" or "female" sticker would be attached to each bag. We would get people to donate the individual parts of the gifts, and then we would give these to Steve, who would assemble them into the packages that needed to be wrapped.

Steve and Ellen went the extra mile in helping to get the items ready for shipment. They had several other volunteers meet at their home twice every week, where they sorted and bagged hundreds of gifts. The Godziks converted the basement of their home into a workshop for their crew, and these OTS volunteers came to be known as the "Cellar Dwellers." They did a superb job preparing hundreds of gifts to be sent overseas.

Cellar Dwellers

Cellar Dwellers

It is truly amazing how much one can accomplish when a few people work together. The Cellar Dwellers made some wonderful things happen, and hundreds of deployed soldiers benefitted from their efforts.

Branching Out

We were sending care packages every day and conducting Christmas wraps on a regular basis. The FSG meetings were well attended, and the families were greeted by professionals from all types of specialties. We thought the one area that could be expanded was to do projects that would involve the families. This approach would keep them occupied during the deployment and put them in an environment where they could relate to others coping with the same stress level. We began to plan for events that would fill this need.

Yard Sale

We decided to start our list of projects with a yard sale. We have all been involved with yard sales in the past and thought this one shouldn't be much different. Right? Let's say it was a bit more than we had imagined.

We made up flyers and posted them around town. We advertised our intentions in the local newspaper. We spread the word whenever and wherever we went, and as the day of the sale got closer, we used a box truck to pick up items from individuals, businesses, churches, schools, and any other place that called, such as a farm in New Hampshire that had old furniture in their barn for us. We drove around and picked up items until nine or ten at night and stored them at Easi Storage in Salem, Massachusetts, where the units were donated by the manager, Donna Gay, a wonderful friend who truly believed in the OTS cause.

One of our volunteers, Donna Vallis, was a huge help by going to the storage unit constantly, separating out the items, estimating the value, and pricing what she could. This was a monumental task, considering the number of items to be checked. Christine and I would drive over to Salem to see how Donna was doing, and we almost could not find her behind the mountains of donated furniture, clothes, kitchenware, books, toys, and all sorts of other miscellaneous items. Donna had some help on an interim basis, and they checked each item to ensure it was in good enough shape to sell; then they estimated a price for us. Whatever Donna could not do, we would do the day of the sale.

We had reserved the large parking lot across from the Danvers Town Hall, and all the items were dropped off at that location the night before—just about an hour before it started to rain. In a panic, we threw tarps all over the goods and prayed that the wind would not pick up. Luckily, the rain stopped after a short attack, but it made the setup the next morning that much more challenging.

The items that had been collected consisted of more clothing than one could imagine, all kinds of books, kitchen utensils, several desks, dressers, kitchen tables with chairs, a complete dining room set (table with eight chairs), several living room chairs, a china cabinet, refrigerator, freezer, stereo sets, a "coffin" (which turned out to be a beautiful grandfather clock), and a huge selection of tapes, CDs, cassettes, and even a few vinyl records.

Trying to price everything was tough, and I'm sure we let some treasures go at a tremendous bargain to the buyer. One of the Boston radio stations had heard of our event and came to us with their equipment and a table set up under a tent to broadcast on location. They gave us a lot of air time for the Boston area to hear, and they gave away free keepsakes. They also gave OTS a great review at the end of the day. They had a hard time believing that a volunteer group's yard sale could have so many items and draw such a huge crowd. We did too. At the end of the day, we had made over $12,000 for our postage. This was one special yard sale.

There were, however, a few not-so-good occurrences during the day. We had a clearly marked radio that was to be used to play some background music during the sale, but that was missing at the end of the yard sale. In addition, we had nine working television sets for sale, and one person bought them all. He returned later in the day, telling us that he wanted his money back because none of the sets worked. We had a difficult time believing this, as every one of them had been checked in the morning, but since he was adamant, we agreed to return his money if he brought the sets back to us. He said they were at his house, and he would not go home to get them. We did not return the money under his conditions, and later, we found that he was a television repair man. I guess we knew why he needed the sets.

One incident worth mentioning occurred when a man hovered around a couple of old, rusty Coca-Cola signs that had been used at the old-time gas stations; he saw that we had a price tag of thirty dollars each on them. He knew that the items were worth far more than thirty dollars. When a lady offered fifteen dollars, he stepped in and offered to pay the thirty dollars to avoid a further loss to OTS. Our yard sale was in July. Nearly three months later, we were setting up our information booth at the Topsfield Fair, and I saw this same gentleman approach me. He reminded me that he was at the yard sale and had purchased the Coke signs. He knew they were underpriced, so he bought them and sold them on eBay for $150 each. He then proceeded to hand me $300 cash for our postage. I told him that he had purchased the signs at our asking price, but he insisted on giving us the money, saying that it was for the troops, and they were worth the money he received for the items. This was a very special gesture, but it was more common than one would think. What a great feeling, knowing that your country loves you.

Our first Yard Sale

Our first Yard Sale

Due to the success of the first yard sale, OTS organized additional yard sales in the schools and other locations throughout the Danvers area. Unlike the first one, which was out of our control due to the huge number of items for sale and many volunteers who didn't really have a firm grasp of what to do, we were determined to make the next one a little smoother. Our volunteers came forward to organize the event right away, with inventory charts, pricing lists, security protection, cleanup procedures, and—perhaps most important—disposition of remaining items. We had an agreement with a used book company to take our excess books, and because the venue was inside the school, security was much easier to control. The morning of the event was smooth, as we were able to keep the doors locked and the public out until we were ready to go.

This "yard sale" went off smoothly, and we made significant money for our postage that day. We organized follow-on events in the same manner, and we even had a bake sale in the lobby as an added attraction. A few of the events had raffle baskets to award to some lucky ticket holders.

This idea of combining two or three individual sub-events for each of our main projects worked out very well because that attracted a lot more people, continued to get more of our volunteers involved, and brought in more postage money. One yard sale at the middle school attracted one of our town's major automobile dealerships, which parked a beautiful new car at the door for some free advertising and additional attraction to curious townsfolk.

We have had several venues for our yard sales over the years, with schools, public property, and individual homeowners' yards all serving as our hosts. These became popular because the money went to a good cause that everyone could give to. Even when we were not planning for a yard sale, people would call and tell me they had this item or that item, and they would like to contribute it to the next yard sale. This was really heartwarming, but did cause a challenge with storage space. We never minded, though, because for the longest time, this was our biggest postage fundraising event.

New and improved yard sale

Craft Fair

The spirit was catching hold, and this prompted some of our volunteers to suggest other initiatives to broaden our reach and connect to new people in need of our help. One of our volunteers also suggested that we try a craft fair to raise awareness of OTS and to raise money for our postage expense. Many of them were gifted in making craft items or knew someone who could help us out. Not being too familiar with how to oversee a craft fair, we spoke to those who had experience in this type of event and then began our planning. The general idea was to rent out a space to the craft person, who then would bring his or her table and products. Then, they would sell their items and keep any profit they made. It was a relatively simple concept.

The day of the event arrived, and it was amazing to see the absolutely beautiful treasures that went on sale—from dolls, to clocks, to plants, to house decorations and holiday ornaments. That day, we came in contact with a lot of people who had not previously worked with us, and it was evident that this diversified approach was working.

The craft fair did something else. Many of the family members who had come to OTS seeking some comfort during their loved ones' absences started to concentrate on a talent they themselves had, and this led to a healthy distraction from the sadness and constant fear with which they were living. They started to focus on their own skills, and this was a very good way to get through the day. In addition, the knowledge of these talents gave us more avenues to pursue when our future raffle events came up, for we had discovered an excellent source of items to raffle to the public.

The OTS Craft Fair

Plant Sale

The yard sales and craft fair had worked out well. One day we received a call from the owners of the Cressy Greenhouses in Rowley, Massachusetts. They asked me if we might be interested in having a plant sale, since Mother's Day was approaching, and it would be a good time to buy a plant for Mom. This appealed to me, as I usually bought Christine flowers or a plant for Mother's Day, so I made the command decision to give it a try. Here's how it would work: the nursery would bring the plants down to us in the morning, along with an inventory and a list of the prices that OTS would pay the nursery at the end of the event. In addition, they gave us a list of recommended prices for sale to the public. It was our choice of whether to use the suggested retail price or make our own list.

We spread the flowers and plants over the area we had been allotted, and they looked really rich and beautiful to the people driving by. Since that first plant sale, we have had many over time, and the recommended pricing that came from the nursery was usually the best choice. At the end of the day, the nursery would return, count up the number of plants remaining, and simply charge us for the number sold. Then they would take back the unsold items. Safe, clean, simple, and we always made a profit for doing a minimum amount of work.

The thing about a plant sale, as with any event that you hold for the public, is that you want to be in a location where people can see you. Our advertising would bring a lot of people out, especially at that time of the year—close to Mother's Day and in the springtime, when people start thinking of brightening up their yards for the good weather. Many people who drive by but who have no intention of buying a plant may be spurred into stopping once they see the beautiful arrangements and suspect that Mom would love them forever if they surprised her on her special day.

The town of Danvers had its town hall at an intersection of two of the town's busiest roads. There was a small parking space and grassy area directly in front of the building, and everyone knew where it was when they read the advertisement or heard about it. I thought that would be an excellent spot to display the plants, so I went down to the town hall to ask permission for OTS to set up on the Saturday morning of Mother's Day weekend. After bringing it up to the higher powers and checking to ensure no other work was scheduled for that day, they called and told me to go ahead.

This turned out to be a wonderful spot, as all drivers had to slow down or stop at the intersection, giving them a good look at the beautiful plants and triggering their minds to bring home a flower. We made a couple of large signs, ran off several price lists, picked one cashier to handle the cash box, and made a list to record which plants were sold. In addition, we asked for volunteers to work the yard—setting up the plants, rearranging the items as other plants sold, straightening the inventory for better viewing, and so on. The morning flew by, with a lot of visitors willing to spend a few dollars for a nice potted plant or seasonal vegetable. We had the initial delivery of plants at 9:00 a.m., and at 1:00 p.m., the truck returned to pick up the remaining inventory. The driver made a quick count of what was left, and we paid the price that was in our agreement. What was left was several hundred dollars for the OTS post office fund—and a good time for the volunteers.

Our OTS Plant Sale

Trip to a Water Park

The yard sales, craft fair, and plant sales were carried out to bring volunteers together to raise postage money, but the families needed something more to raise their comfort level during their loved ones' deployments. Over the next few years, we set up outings for the families to keep their spirits up.

One afternoon we reserved several hours at a water sport park called CoCo Key, where the families could enjoy water slides, a swimming pool, a snack bar, and other games. This was a nice diversion from the daily worries that abounded in the families while they awaited the return of their loved ones. This was one more way of keeping their minds off the pain of separation.

Trip to Boston

It's really amazing, setting up the activities for the families. Everyone had a great time, and the families started to suggest other events that might be fun for the group. Someone recommended a day trip into Boston. That sounded great but also fairly complicated. I said I would see what we could do. Contacting the Boston Trolleys and Fenway Park, I set up a wonderful day trip to Boston in which many family members took part. This outing included a visit to Boston and a guided tour of the state capital. We started our day with a trolley tour of Boston, including the trip to the capitol building; a visit to the Boston Public Gardens; and a great "duck tour" of the Charles River, where our land vehicle went crashing into the River Charles, and suddenly, we found ourselves floating on the waterways of historic Boston.

When at last we came off the river, we were dropped off at Fenway Park, home of the World Series champion Boston Red Sox. The park was closed, so we had the whole stadium to ourselves. We enjoyed sitting in the broadcasters' booth, waving from the Green Monster seats in left field, and standing beside the specially marked seat where Ted Williams's 502-foot home run landed. This was the longest home run in Red Sox history, and the ball bounced off the head of a Mr. Joseph Boucher of Albany, New York, during a Red Sox/Tigers game. Today, that seat is painted red in a sea of green seats in the surrounding area. It seems sad that Mr. Boucher didn't get to keep the ball. Following the tour of Fenway, we all ate at one of the popular lunch establishments, and then we headed home. This was one outing we remembered for a long time.

OTS Volunteers at Fenway Park

Fenway Park, Boston, MA

Speaking of Fenway Park, we received a letter from a marine lance corporal stationed at Al Asaad, Iraq. He explained that he was a Red Sox fan from Massachusetts, and his roommate was a staunch New York Yankees fan. They were always taunting each other, and when the young marine saw that we were from the Boston area, he wrote to us and requested that we send a Red Sox item to his roommate as a humorous gesture to gain a reaction. When we received his letter, we decided to treat our Red Sox fan to a really big show. We bought a Red Sox shirt, a Red Sox ball cap, signed pictures of the team and some of individual players, a Red Sox video, photos of Fenway Park, and a "Beat the Yankees" sticker for him to put on his wall.

A few weeks later, we received a letter from our Red Sox marine. He said the package came just as the Red Sox had beaten the Yankees. His roommate had some colorful language to share as he opened up his timely gifts. Our fan smugly told him that when you mess around with Red Sox nation, you have to suffer the consequences. He told us that we had made his day.

Godzik Picnics

As the years went on, Steve and Ellen Godzik decided to give a day to our volunteers by hosting a picnic in their backyard. This old-fashioned family outing was just what we all needed to kick back, not travel anywhere, and chat with friends about life, hobbies, the support for the troops, and so on. Any topic was allowed, and we all took advantage of the hospitality. Steve played the role of chef and cooked up hot dogs, hamburgers, steak tips, and anything else that the folks would bring from home. On occasion, Bob Bent shared the cooking duties, while the adults as well as the children had a swim in the Godzik pool. Since Steve was a gardener, we had the good fortune of picking the ripe tomatoes, squash, strawberries, and a host of other farm-fresh products straight from the garden. The Godziks had a permanent tent in their yard, so even if the day was cloudy or rainy, we still all loved getting together at the "Godzik picnic," one of the year's most enjoyable events.

There were times when we used the picnic to invite the families of soldiers who had been injured so that they could be around friends at a very difficult time. In one instance, the recovering son was in a hospital down South, and the parents had to travel back and forth to see him—a very expensive situation. We all chipped in and bought some plane tickets to ease the burden, and it was very much appreciated. That's one way to take care of your brothers and sisters when the times get rough. Over the years, Steve and Ellen were not able to continue hosting this wonderful party, but the memories will live on in the minds and hearts of everyone.

OTS Family Picnic
at the Godziks

Relaxing day at the OTS picnic

Independence Day Celebrations

Our Independence Day celebration came at the July 4 fireworks at the Plains Park in Danvers. OTS had set up several tables at the park, and each year we were one of the earliest parties to assemble, arriving around 10:00 a.m. on July 3 to set up. As the day went on, more and more of our family members came and joined in the fun. There were vendors, games, and handouts everywhere at the park, and we had a wonderful time celebrating as a community. Later in the day, as the sun set and the night skies began to set in, the town would call us to the field to open up the military portion of the evening. Each year, I would act as the master of ceremonies and welcome the hundreds, even thousands, of guests. I would ask all of the veterans in the area to stand and be recognized. At this time, patriotic music would play—usually the service songs of each military branch—and fathers, mothers, brothers, sisters, grandmothers, grandfathers, and aunts and uncles would all stand and wave the American flag, all proud of their heritage, all proud to be Americans.

As I finished my introductions, the army parachute team would drop from the sky, carrying with them the United States flag, waving proudly in the night sky. What a beautiful sight! Our town was celebrating, and we loved it. On most nights, we were even blessed with a flyover of military fighters, which, as one can imagine, set the crowd cheering and waving their flags. Then, as the darkness set in, the fireworks would begin. The fireworks team had been doing this for years, and people were never disappointed. The show was nearly equal to the celebration on Boston's esplanade, lighting up the sky with a background of patriotic music. Our families loved every minute of it and went home at the end of the night feeling a little prouder of their loved ones serving so many miles away.

The very next morning, we were at it again, traveling over to Patton Park in Hamilton, Massachusetts. A day-long celebration was about to begin, and we set up our canopies for hours of family festivities. Attendees included the Army Reserve, Boy and Girl Scouts, and groups from throughout the town displaying their products, usually with a patriotic influence. There was a beautiful parade and food everywhere. On most days, Mrs. Joanne Patton was part of the OTS table, and sometimes her son and grandsons would join us. Those were wonderful days that live on in our memories.

Auction

One day, one of our volunteers recommended that we try running an auction. None of us had ever tried this type of fundraiser, but we were willing to look into it. We were introduced to a wonderful person named Nicole Grace, who had a lot of experience with auctions, and she was willing to organize the event for OTS. Nicole assembled a team consisting of her and Linda Boisclair as cochairs, along with a committee of Lori Barlow, Marcia Colella, and Alexis Gilbode. This team put together a remarkable event. The auction was held in the grand ballroom of the Holiday Inn and Suites in Peabody, Massachusetts. Over 250 live and silent auction items were donated. These prizes consisted of jewelry, restaurant gift cards, autographed sports memorabilia, ski passes, a resort stay, overnight hotel stays, one hundred gallons of home heating oil, a full CSA (Community Supported Agriculture) share at Patton's Green Meadows Farm, original artwork, handmade blankets, museum passes, spa treatments, and New England Patriots tickets.

Each gift was covered in colored transparent paper and placed in a basket or box, giving the prizes a beautiful appearance, and set on long tables, with signs and clipboards for bidding. In addition, there were other tables and chairs in the room to allow the guests to sit and take part in the live auction or relax while deciding what to bid on. The presentation was superb, and the overall event was absolutely first class. In addition, ten restaurants donated food for the attendees to eat during their visit.

The final income generated by this auction was $17,850, a remarkable achievement by a remarkable team. Nicole and Linda and the committee members deserved a huge vote of recognition for a job extremely well done.

Nicole Grace (center) inspecting the auction items

Carol Slavin at the auction

The OTS Dinner

Looking back to 2004, at the one-year anniversary of our founding, we thought it would be nice to hold a dinner to say thank you to our volunteers for helping throughout the year. This was a small event at the Danvers VFW hall, and we made it a potluck supper. When we finished eating, Christine and I handed out certificates of appreciation to everyone who had given their time over the past twelve months. Each year thereafter, we held a similar dinner in the spring to celebrate the OTS volunteers. Over time, these dinners became larger, and the certificates became plaques. We paid for the early dinners and certificates, as we wanted to use all of the donated money for the care packages. In time, however, we decided to charge a fee for the dinner through the sale of tickets to help defray the cost. The room at the VFW had a maximum attendee limit of eighty, and we found that it wasn't large enough to hold the number of people who wanted to attend, so we looked for a venue that could accommodate a larger guest list.

We moved to the middle school cafeteria, then to the Vittori Rocci Italian American/AMVETS post in Beverly. When we outgrew that post, we chose a larger, more formal setting at Timothy's (now called Breakaway) on Route 1 in Danvers. Finally, we moved into Angelica's in Middleton, capacity about 250 people. We remained there until the beautiful function room was shut down during the pandemic, from 2020 to 2022. We loved Angelica's, and we hosted many first-class events that kept people talking all year. These dinners were catered events, with flowers, plaques for honorees, formal military color guards, guest speakers, entertainers, movies showing the OTS events of the past year, and—above all else—a beautiful tribute to the men and women who sacrificed their lives by representing America in a war-torn foreign country. Volunteers, families, friends, military units, politicians, and clergy all came to this one place to pay tribute to America, and it was a beautiful tribute.

Some of our guest speakers at the annual dinner included a Medal of Honor recipient, a World War II Iwo Jima survivor, a POW who became a painter and expressed his ordeal in his works, and an air force doctor who ran the Boston Marathon on the day of the Boston bombing, then left the finish line and ran to his hospital down the street, where he operated on the victims for thirty-seven straight hours. In addition, marine sergeant Dan Clark, the singing trooper, was tremendous with his patriotic music.

The OTS annual dinner was a fun-filled evening, where people could get together for a common purpose—to honor the soldiers who were deployed. This, above all else, was the objective of the night, and all the decorations, flowers, raffle items, and music were added to enhance the joy of the event. All year, we were concerned about the safety of our loved ones, and for this one night, we celebrated each other as faithful Americans, supporting the decisions of our country, and enjoying the time with friends and family.

The OTS Dinner at Angelicas

Behind The Scenes

Most people see Operation Troop Support as a charitable organization that sends care packages and Christmas gifts to the soldiers throughout the year. Under our supervision, the public will pack three hundred or four hundred boxes in a single morning's event. At the end of the day, our OTS trailer is full of care packages, ready to add postage labels and send to the troops. The troops receive the gifts one to two weeks later. While this is an accurate assessment of what happens for a packing or wrapping event, other actions need to take place to make the process work. Let's look at what we do to bring these items to the public and show how they end up in Iraq, Afghanistan, Kuwait, Qatar, the UAE, Poland, Romania, Bulgaria, Nigeria, Djibouti, and several other countries far, far away.

Record Keeping

The number of soldiers to whom we send packages requires us to keep accurate records. This begins when we first receive a request to send the items. This request can come directly from the soldier or from a family member or even another one of our troops. Christine has organized a system for cataloging each recipient by name, full mailing address, date that we received the request, and any additional information, such as anticipated return date. We photocopy the request and attach it to a name label for the troop. Each time a package is sent out, we annotate the label with the date and number of packages sent. The mailing list needs to be managed closely to ensure every soldier gets a box and that all soldiers receive a package on a rotating basis. The daily influx of requests, coupled with the notices that soldiers are rotating out, or switching locations, or returning early make this a difficult challenge, and Christine is on constant watch for situations that require updating the files.

As our packages begin reaching the soldiers, additional men and women stationed with them ask for items as well. In addition, some requests come in with six or seven names attached. A mechanism that we use to add new soldiers to the database is the Care Package Request (CPR) form, described earlier. This form may be used for one or multiple names, and we get two or more of these completed CPRs every week.

Donations

In addition to the record keeping, the handling of donations is another very important task that takes hours of effort. OTS has researched the postal codes and transportation laws, along with security and safety rules, to ensure we adhere to the appropriate guidelines for sending our packages to the various countries. We check all of the donated items to make sure the products are not outdated. We are very careful to send products that have not yet reached their expiration date, and this process takes a long time. It is very important that we treat each soldier in the best manner that we can, and this means giving them fresh and current items. Our rules prohibit our sending alcohol, pork, or inappropriate reading or viewing materials. Glass also is not allowed, due to the chance of breakage in flight.

The donations are split between food items, toiletries, and other miscellaneous materials. From experience, we learned never to pack food in the same box as toiletries. Early in our existence, a soldier's care package was returned to us because the soldier left his station before his time was up. When we opened it to inspect the contents, *we noted that many of the food items had picked up the scent of toiletries packed in the same box, and this solidified our resolve to keep food and toiletries separated.*

The largest challenge behind the scenes in preparing for a pack or wrap is in storing the donated items until the day of the event. Individuals and organizations would bring boxes or bags of goods to us that needed to be sorted and bagged, and we needed a place to put the donated items before we began the preparation of the package.

When we receive food products, these are shipped out right away so that they reach their destination while still within their freshness dates. Many of the toiletries and other nonfood items, however, may have to be stored for a short period before being sent out. To the extent we can fit them into our OTS trailer, this is a good storage solution, but if the trailer's capacity is exceeded, we need some other short-term storage options. Cranney Storage of Danvers and Easi Space of Salem, Massachusetts, have been wonderful in this regard. Both organizations have exhibited their patriotism by donating units for temporary storage needs. Some examples of items that have exceeded our immediate needs are puzzle books, socks, and toothbrushes and toothpaste.

In addition, we need to be ready to accept donations from all sources. A nonprofit organization out of Michigan called Cards for Soldiers has been sending cards to us to forward to the soldiers for the past few years. Hundreds of these packages of cards are received every day, and we are delighted to assist them in their mission to help the troops. In addition, for years the Paradies Shops from Portland, Maine, has sent multiple cartons of miscellaneous items each week to help us fill out our care packages. These items are all new and very useful to the soldiers. Other repeat contributors include a multitude of churches, schools, retirement communities, civic organizations, and businesses that keep our volunteers very busy each day. The USO has been a great help, and they pass many donations our way when they are unable to handle them.

One day, we received a telephone call, and the caller asked where our "warehouse" was located. Not thinking much about it, I gave the directions to our home, from which we run the OTS. About twenty minutes later, an eighteen-wheel trailer truck pulled up in front of my driveway. The driver stepped out and opened the truck's back doors. He then took a forklift from the truck and downloaded two full shrink-wrapped pallets of some product and placed them in the middle of our driveway. We were not accustomed to this type of delivery, but we thanked the driver, who went on his way.

The products had come from a company in Indiana, and luckily, I had my grandson there to help me count the items—these were small tubes of product, each enclosed in a separate box. After a few hours, we realized that we had been delivered fifty-nine thousand tubes of Anti Monkey Butt diaper rash cream. I wasn't sure what we would do with thousands of tubes of this cream, but we started sending these overseas to the units.

Within two weeks, I started getting feedback. The troops wanted to know where we got this cream. *It is awesome. Send us more.* This feedback was not from just one unit but several at different locations. The cream contained calamine lotion and other moisture-absorbing ingredients that the soldiers needed. I felt we had hit the lottery, and we started sending more to the troops. Before long, we had exhausted our supply, and I found myself doing something I never thought I would do—calling the company and asking for more. They followed up with recommendations on their powders and other products, and we ordered several different items, all of which were very happily received by the soldiers. That incident taught us to accept all donations with open arms.

Over the years, we have received donations from across the country. One day, I traveled to California, where a company generously donated multiple sets of bed sheets. Another day, we received several boxes from Wyoming, where the organization paid nearly $100 in postage just to send the items to us. A very nice lady called the White House to see how she could get a care package to her grandson in the Middle East. They told her to contact Operation Troop Support. We were surprised when she told us this, but then we found out that our state senator had just had lunch with the vice president, and the senator told him about us. I was amazed that we were so well known!

After the sorting, bagging, packing, and paperwork has been completed for the day, Christine and I assess what we need for the next day's packages. If we need items to augment our donation inventory, we make a list of items at the dollar store or one of the other discount outlets. These items are used to give our soldiers some enjoyment during their downtime. Puzzle books, playing cards, pens, crossword puzzle books, and so on fill this need. Christine or I make a trip to get these articles, or we ask the Godziks or one of our other volunteers to go on the errand. Having a volunteer take care of our shopping list is a big help when these services are needed.

Supplies

Over time, OTS acquired a lot of small but required assets, such as tape and tape guns, mailing boxes, and Ziploc bags, which we kept in our storage facilities or our home until needed. In addition, we had pop-up canopy tents to bring to outings. These tents allowed us to display our items and advertise our needs without the rain or direct sunlight interfering with us.

Sandwich boards helped us with our advertising at large events, and we had to store a speaker system, which we used at larger venues. Raffle baskets were kept in storage at Cranney's or Easi Storage when not in use, and our OTS shirts and hats also were stored at these locations. Tables for displaying our items were there, along with several folding chairs for our volunteers.

We also kept our Christmas wrapping paper, scissors, shipping tape, Christmas tags, and extra packing boxes at these facilities. Travel to and from these storage units created a special challenge because in addition to the time spent in going to the unit, we needed to take the items out, which often required multiple trips, plus put everything back at the end of the day.

A Trailer Comes Our Way

As the years went by and OTS became busier, we had a growing need to have a place for our supplies and packing items when we went to and from our packing venues. A packing event required all the items to pack, plu s the postage boxes, packing tape, and dispensers, and we were relying on borrowed box trucks to fill this requirement.

That all came to an end when one of our volunteers, Rob O'Keefe, came to us one day and told us he was going to do his annual walk for OTS and wanted to know if we needed anything in particular, in addition to postage money. We told him of our need for a trailer or van to move our items. He said he would use the money for that purpose if he raised enough, and that's exactly what he did.

He went down to Cap World, and purchased a beautiful black cargo trailer. We had printing done on all sides to show our organization to the world. It worked out so well that we were able to carry all the supplies for a pack within its space. We were so pleased that Rob had suggested an alternate use for the money he was about to raise. Anyone donating funds to OTS can be assured the money will go to the postage, but Rob had raised his money for a specific purpose to help out the organization, and we were thrilled to be able to do it.

The trailer donated by Rob O'Keefe

The Giving Tree

Several years went by, and OTS was asked if we would like to use a Christmas tree in the Liberty Tree Mall in Danvers to function as a giving tree for gifts to send to the soldiers. The locals loved the idea. They would take a paper ornament off the tree, which contained the name of an item needed by a soldier. They would then purchase the gift and turn it in to the mall security office, where OTS then would take it and send it to the appropriate soldier. This was a wonderful way to allow the public to join in our mission of helping the troops.

One day, Christine was down at the mall, taking pictures of the giving tree, and a lady came up to her and started to talk about the purpose of the tree. She explained that she worked in the customer outreach department of the Volvo dealership across the street from the mall, and they were looking for something to do for the community. She was so impressed with what we were doing that she asked what we needed. Christine said we were in need of another trailer, as we had outgrown the first one. They parted ways, and Christine didn't think much more about the conversation—until the next day, when that same lady called her. She said she had brought it up to management, and they thought it would be a perfect way to give to the town. We had a second trailer within a few days, and we made sure the Volvo dealership had its name on the sides so the town of Danvers knew of their kindness. This was a wonderful thing to do for the US military.

Trailer donated by Volvo Village of Danvers, MA

Another facet of our work behind the scenes involves having the appropriate paperwork, pamphlets, stickers, and give-away items ready to bring to an event. We also need to plan appropriate advertising for any upcoming event.

More and more opportunities started to come our way as the months turned into years, and this required additional work behind the scenes. Flyers were needed that advertised upcoming packs and wraps, as well as Facebook announcements and newspaper articles showing the future yard sales, craft fairs, plant sales, bike runs, FSG meetings, and other events. Paperwork needed to be generated to let everyone know that OTS had something planned.

The evenings were filled with speaking engagements at churches, civic groups, and Scout meetings, and daytime meetings were devoted to retirement homes and nursing facilities. In between, we unloaded donations, sorted, and bagged items, and wrote thank-you notes to every single person or group who had given us a contribution. Since I was holding down a full-time job in international contracting, I was often pulled away, and this created a challenge to Christine and me to get the OTS needs met.

Another facet of the behind-the-scenes part of our job was the outreach program. In addition to the scores of telephone calls that came in daily requesting information on what to donate, calls consistently requested that we send someone to talk to their group about our organization and discuss how they could help out. Civic groups, businesses, churches, Scout troops, retirement communities, YMCAs, schools, and other entities wanted me to explain how we were helping the soldiers. We had interesting anecdotes to relate, and these stories excited the groups and got them ready to help out. These visits gave us a sense of real satisfaction, and we looked forward to doing as many as we could. They were very taxing, however, and had to be curtailed somewhat as the years went on.

At one point, a billboard company came to me and asked if we would be interested in having a couple of billboards erected that suggested people remember the soldiers and donate to OTS. Since it was the Christmas season, we thought the idea was good, and several billboards went up—at no charge to us—along the main streets and highways around Danvers, advertising our mission. There's an odd feeling driving down the street and seeing a huge billboard telling people to contact you.

One thing about the human spirit is that when you do something good, it makes you feel good. This was never so noticeable as when people donated to OTS. Everyone was so friendly, and those with family or friends in the military had a story to tell about their experiences or where they were stationed. Donating to a military support organization brings out the best in people, and it makes our job that much more rewarding.

As OTS became known to more and more military organizations, we were asked for our challenge coin. A military unit is recognized by a unique coin that identifies the holder with a particular organization, and it is usually given by a unit commander in recognition of a special achievement or to prove membership in an organization. The more places we went, the more the military or government representatives gave us their coins in recognition of the work we were doing with the troops. We finally decided to obtain our own to hand out to people and units who we felt deserved the honor.

I had met a coin company manager at a VFW convention and told her that we were thinking of getting a challenge coin for OTS. After discussing with me some ideas on potential designs for a coin, her company, 4Heroes, sent us potential sign proofs, and we selected a beautiful pattern that fit our purpose. We ordered several hundred of these coins, and for years we were able to give them to the military personnel at meetings, conventions, patriotic events and other gatherings. People not in the military could purchase the coins as a way to show support. The OTS coin was more than an organizational showpiece; it was the symbol of the group that took care of our soldiers and their families. Our volunteers were so proud to hand them out.

As the years went on, we used 4Heroes to make us a tenth anniversary pin, as well as a fifteenth anniversary pin. These were very popular at our care-package events and became a source of income for our organization, along with the challenge coin, in an effort to make postage money.

The OTS Challenge Coin

We decided to add more handouts to give to interested people. We printed up a multiple-page pamphlet showing the different types of activities with which OTS is involved. In addition, we printed OTS bumper stickers and some other stickers to put onto cars or books.

Incorporation

As we grew larger, many people asked us if we were a 501(c) (3) IRS approved nonprofit organization, and finally, we took steps to incorporate. Contacting the IRS, we received their instructions and submitted the required paperwork. They required us to write a mission statement, and we elected a board of directors, filled out the organization's policies and procedures, set up the required banking system, and had the specific submittals made. We received our Federal ID number and received authorization to do business as an IRS-approved nonprofit corporation. That was in 2007, and we have operated under this umbrella ever since.

The formal IRS nonprofit designation has given us greater status among potential grant opportunities, and for this, I feel gratitude. Most companies who are willing to donate funding require a tax ID number, and our nonprofit number has been a great help in securing grants and other contributions. Banks, larger corporations, and charitable foundations have all requested our nonprofit number prior to donating any money. Of course, it is very important to be able to show the nonprofit status at tax season as well.

OTS Becomes the Post Office

The post office representative showed me how to use a postal program. It is wonderful. With this program, I can print out our mailing labels, secure them onto the boxes, and send them out without having to bring them to the post office. Every day, the post office comes to my house and picks up the packages, and the postage fee is deducted from the OTS bank account. This is a great program.

The above activities show the different facets of running the organization. It involves planning, organizing, storing supplies, transporting goods, advertising our mission, taking this mission to the community, supervising the public packs and holiday wraps, and making sure everyone who donated an item receives our note of appreciation for their generosity. It's a challenging job, but the rewards are definitely worth it as we recognize that our behind-the-scenes efforts are bringing happiness into the life of a soldier, sailor, airman, or marine. We wouldn't trade it for the world.

OTS Reaches The Community

As the years passed, it seemed that everyone was eager to help the troops through OTS, and the more we were able to reach the public, the more the public pitched in to help in the cause. Some of the more noticeable examples of how people responded to the OTS mission are worthy of mention here.

Jimmy George

One person came forward to show his support in a very unusual way. Mr. Jim George, a retired Danvers police officer and Korean War army veteran, wanted to do something special, so he made a sign, asking for donations for OTS, and stood on the sidewalk in Danvers Square one Saturday morning. The public was so eager to help that Jim returned to his post the next Saturday, and the next. For the next twelve years, rain or shine, weekends or holidays, Jimmy was out in the middle of Danvers Center, collecting for the troops. He became such a fixture on the corner that it seemed odd on those few days when he had to miss. He became one of the most popular people in town and developed a huge following, from the younger generation to the elderly, who remembered him from his days as a cop walking his beat in town.

Vendors in the town brought him coffee on cold days and cool drinks in the summer. People from all over the North Shore of Boston knew of Jimmy George and, in turn, found out about Operation Troop Support. It was a win-win situation. I used to go down to the square to talk to him during his time on station, and he was so happy to see me. He loved his job, and he relished the time he spent with the folks he called "my people." Everybody loved Jimmy, and when he passed away, the whole town went into mourning.

Christina-Marie Moody & Jimmy George in Danvers Square

The impact of Jimmy's unselfish efforts was clearly seen on many occasions as we began getting letters from the troops, telling us just how much the items that he had collected meant to them. For example, one day we received a note from the soldiers attached to the 382nd Military Police Battalion in central Iraq. They had received our packages full of gifts and cards before Christmas. They gave them out to their soldiers at their holiday meals, get-togethers, and while standing guard in the desert on Christmas Eve. They explained what it meant to the soldiers and told us that for the moment, through our kindness, they were able to sense the pureness of our act—gifts, carefully wrapped and labeled, from someone they did not know and who did not know them. They told us that they would never forget what we had done to brighten up their melancholy day.

Jimmy approached me one day and said he wanted to organize a walk for the troops. We loved the idea, and soon he had outlined a route, a date, and a time for the event to take place. He also invited a surprise guest to walk with him, Boston Bruins great Terry O'Reilly, one of the most famous Bruins players in the history of Boston sports. Terry earned the reputation of being the heart and soul of the Bruins and was the undisputed hardest-hitting hockey player in town. When he showed up the day of the walk, people came out to see the Boston great, to speak to him, and to get an autograph. Terry took part in more than one of our walks because he was truly behind the soldiers and wanted to show the colors when he had the opportunity.

Christine & Terry O'Reilly signing autographs at the OTS walk

It was very difficult to estimate Jimmy's worth to the group or the town because for every dollar he collected, he inspired so many people to give to the cause.

Support from the Townsfolk

Everyone was getting into the spirit. A twelve-year-old boy sold lemonade, with the proceeds going to the troops; a 102-year-old great-grandmother, at one of our Christmas events, helped wrap gifts to send to the soldiers. The number of care packages and the destination locations continued to expand faster than we had imagined.

A staunch supporter of OTS over the years was Rob O'Keefe, who had donated the cargo trailer to us and came to nearly every event we had. Rob approached me one day and asked if we would accept the proceeds from a walk that he planned to do around Christmas. We were delighted by his request, and he followed up by announcing the event to his business networking group. This had an immediate impact in sponsorship donations. Rob has done a walk every year for the troops and has brought in over $50,000 through his efforts.

As time passed, more and more people began to contact us, bringing us items to ship out, and visiting our Family Support Group meetings. Some soldiers returned home, and they were willing to speak to our group on their experiences and their needs. At nine o'clock on New Year's morning, a knock on our door brought me face-to-face with a young marine, who thanked me for all the packages our group had sent him during his deployment. He said it made a huge difference and helped his unit get through the year with their spirits raised. They knew that people from their homeland cared. That was an emotional meeting, but it propelled us into the new year with the hope that we might be making a difference. We couldn't wait to keep it going.

Town Fathers Help Out

Visits to some schools and Scouting organizations gave us the opportunity to expand our outreach activities. We organized two community walks to raise awareness of the soldiers' needs, and we introduced a bill to the town, which was subsequently approved by the Danvers Board of Selectmen to grant deferments of utility bills to families while their loved ones were serving in the desert.

Grants

By the time we had been sending our care packages for a couple of years, people began suggesting ways to obtain grants for our postage. A lady who came to one of our packs at the Brooksby Village Senior Living Community recommended that I fill out an application for a grant from the Ruby Linn Foundation. This lady was a board member on the foundation, which was named for an officer in the US Army, who had been a director at Walter Reed Medical Center in Washington, DC. Ruby Linn and her husband began a charitable foundation to help organizations to make a better living standard for Americans.

I immediately completed the required paperwork, and within two weeks, we were notified that the board had approved a $10,000 grant to OTS to help with our postage expenses under our care-package program. This was such a blessing to us; as it turned out, this was the first of several annual grants from this foundation. In addition, we received grants from Eastern Bank and a large contribution from the Danvers Savings Bank.

These grants were wonderful and kept us going during the early years, but the steady stream of twenty-dollar and fifty-dollar checks that showed up in our mail each day were a godsend and provided us with the funding necessary to ship a lot of our packages. This gesture showed us how much the American public cared for their troops. Once we were set up on the internet and had a website, donations started coming in from across the country. We received contributions from Colorado, Wisconsin, Florida, California, New York, and Arizona, to name just a few of the states.

As the years went on, more and more organizations reached out to us, asking what they could do to help us. We always told them which items were requested by the troops, and we would add that our postage expense always needed a monetary contribution. It was always a great thing to welcome different organizations onto the OTS team.

Cards for Soldiers

One day, we received a telephone call from Cards for Soldiers, a group out of Michigan, and they asked us to help them send their beautiful handmade cards to the troops. We were happy to work with them, and this started a friendship. Their organization sent us four to five very large boxes of newly designed cards every few weeks for years. The cards were truly beautiful, and we included them in our packages.

At least three huge boxes of donations containing items sold at the airport kiosks came in each month as well.

Parrot Heads of Eastern Massachusetts

Another organization that has been a staunch supporter of OTS over the years has been the Parrot Head Club of Eastern Massachusetts. Since 2013, they have consistently run drives for the troops and sponsored raffles, with OTS as the recipient of the proceeds. Over the years, they have raised thousands of dollars for Troop Support, along with hundreds of bags of items to send to the soldiers overseas.

We have grown very fond of the Parrot Heads and hope to continue our partnership in the coming years.

Carol Slavin at the OTS Table with the Parrot Heads

N.E. Patriots' Joe Andruzzi lets Dick wear his Super Bowl Ring at the Parrot Head Convention

Gloucester Veterans

Some of our most active participants are the veterans of Gloucester, Massachusetts. Gloucester has more veterans per capita than any other place in the country, and they show their appreciation for those organizations that care for the troops in many different ways. The Veterans Office in that city is one of the best in the state, and they are always doing an active mission for the soldiers. In addition, the people of Gloucester go out of their way to collect items for OTS.

Ms. Pauline Bresnahan, owner of Gifts by Pauline, a small gift store, is always sponsoring activities, such as Women Vets for the Soldiers, and bringing us huge donations of items and money. It is this kind of community spirit that shows the public that Americans helping Americans is alive and well.

USO

The United Service Organization (USO) continually sent us surplus items, and people as well as organizations would tell us that the USO had recommended that they contact us if any donations were involved.

IRS

One day we received a letter from the IRS. Ordinarily, this would not be a good thing, but in this case, the Internal Revenue Service sent us a monetary donation that their employees had voluntarily contributed. That is the type of IRS letter I like.

From the feedback we received from the soldiers, the unit commanders, the chaplains in the field, and the families back home, OTS was meeting the needs and fulfilling its mission. It was a good thing.

The Topsfield Fair

OTS was moving along at a good pace. Christine and I had turned several rooms in our home into a workshop to handle incoming donations, with tables to sort, pack, and tape outgoing packages; computers and printers to get our mailing labels prepared; and phones to answer the calls from businesses, civic groups, schools, churches, and individuals who wanted to get involved. We loved getting calls from family members who had information on their loved ones who needed our gifts.

We often would reflect on the project we had chosen, and we truly felt as if God was guiding us to do something good for a soldier. More than once, we were told that our package or our interaction with someone had made a big difference in their lives, and this was a wonderful feeling.

Never was this feeling more evident than when we had a booth at the oldest community fair in the country, the Topsfield Fair. Each year, OTS had a station at the fair in October. It was heartwarming to greet the people and hear their stories of when they were in the military or those days during the war when we had helped them contribute to their families in the war zone from the home front. Our presence reminded them of past memories, and several visitors told us how much they enjoyed speaking with us.

At the fair, many of our older-generation volunteers sat at our booth, and the stories that were passed between them and the visitors were wonderful to hear. You could see the sparkle in their eyes as they reminisced about a time gone by. The Topsfield Fair was in town for one week every year, and we enjoyed the time individually and as a group.

Sue Bent talks to visitors at the Topsfield Fair

IN FULL SWING

In April 2005, I was asked to travel to Iraq to assist in the reconstruction program. My previous job in the US Air Force was to handle international contracts, and when I retired and went to work in industry, I did similar work. The government thought that I might be able to assist in training the Iraqi women to take a more active role in the reconstruction effort. These young ladies would come to the States, get a first-rate education at some of the best engineering or management colleges, then go back home to Iraq, where Saddam would not let them work. Now, with the country being freed of that regime, the government wanted to put the reconstruction back into the hands of the Iraqi people whenever possible, and I was asked to help them do it.

As we were approaching Baghdad, the chopper pilot had to do a combat descent due to enemy ground-to-air missiles in the area. The combat descent consisted of very sharp, very fast dives just prior to landing. Being from the air force, I was aware of this tactic, but one person in the helicopter evidently was not. When we started the maneuver, he started screaming, "We've been hit! We're going down! We're going to crash!" As we were in a war zone with missiles flying all over the place, this kind of language was anything but comforting, and we had to take steps to quiet the pilot down—just kidding; it was another passenger. We landed safely, and then it was time to go to work.

After settling in to the quarters set up for me, I toured the various construction sites and saw the buildings that the Army Corps of Engineers had designed and built. These were in varying stages of completion, and the inspection gave me the opportunity to talk to the engineering staff about the challenges that the reconstruction team faced. I met some of the women who were set to take over the work, and I worked with them to teach them about the US government's contracting laws. The women were very intelligent, and proved to be excellent students; they picked up on the rules and procedures very quickly.

Our Blackhawk shortly after touching down in Iraq

One morning, I took the time to visit a combat-support hospital to see what the needs of the patients were. I was sitting on the end of a bed in a room shared by nineteen wounded soldiers in varying degrees of pain. A door opened, and a nurse walked in holding two boxes from Operation Troop Support. I was like a little kid! I jumped up and screamed, "Holy smokes! The system works!" This was an unbelievable moment; seeing how much the items meant to the patients made me tear up with joy. I couldn't wait to get home and tell everyone to keep donating, keep packing, keep shipping out because our men and women truly were inspired by our help.

When I was in country, our son Scott, who was a member of an air force military police unit, and our daughter Tina-Marie, who was an air force combat medic, were in Iraq at the same time. This situation was very challenging for Christine on the home front. She experienced the emotional trauma of being a wife and a mother of deployed family members in a war zone at the same time. Other parents or spouses continued to come to her, requesting guidance on how to cope with the separation of their loved ones, most not realizing she was trying to get through the situation herself. She never let on just how traumatic that time period was for her.

Once I was home, we were able to reconnect with outside agencies and organizations. Following my return, OTS hosted one care-package event, two Christmas wraps, one community walk, and the signing of hundreds of holiday cards, some of which came from the Cards for Soldiers organization. The Catholic Daughters contributed greatly in preparing the Christmas cards for the troops. These cards were for the soldiers from OTS, or they were blank for the troops to sign and send home to their families.

The notes of thanks kept coming in, and this made us believe our work was worth it. One Seabee wrote that our packages meant the world to the morale of the troops, especially those who were on the borders building Iraqi security camps.

As our volunteer list grew, we began to meet every Friday evening at our home to sort and bag donations, pack them into boxes, and fill out the custom forms. Pizza was delivered for everyone, and the night allowed us to help the troops and have a lot of relaxing fun doing it.

The post office offered to let us bring the packages down on Friday night and load them securely on the loading dock, where the postal employees would take care of them first thing Saturday morning. This was a huge help to us, for it allowed all of us, as a group, to move the cargo at a fraction of the time and effort. Our Friday-night packs were not obligatory, but it seemed that everyone wanted to come. Those were fun times that sit in my fond-memory bag. Over the years, many of our volunteers have told me they have missed the camaraderie that developed from that weekly event.

Friday Night packs

Everyone gets into the Act

One day, I called our core volunteers together to discuss how we could make the upcoming year even greater for helping the troops. It was agreed that we needed some fundraising events to get postage money, so we put on our planning hats. The main source would be donations, so we focused on events that would draw people to us to witness the mission firsthand. We planned for some care-packing events, some Christmas wraps, a couple of walks, and an anniversary dinner in the spring to bring the cause to the public.

As we focused our attention on packing the care packages and the Christmas wrapping program, we met some wonderful people along the way. In addition to Brooksby Village, we did wraps at Endicott College, Salem State University, Colby College, the Kiwanis Club, the Lions Club, many senior centers, St. John's Preparatory School, Malden Catholic High School, and several other organizations. We visited the Masons in Salem and hosted Gorton's Seafood from Gloucester, among several other businesses.

We were interviewed by Ms. Lisa Hughes of WBZ, the Boston television station, and Fox News for an interview on the success of our program. We were called to Washington, DC, where we were asked for our opinion on the needs of the military family, and we were asked to sponsor several military children's picnics and Christmas parties of the Massachusetts Army National Guard.

Our number of care packages and Christmas gifts skyrocketed, with the only obstacle being postage money. Our outreach program hit hundreds of people, and our Family Support Group brought in many, many families who needed help, along with excellent speakers, who gave them solace and the assistance they needed to get through the deployment of their loved ones. A note we received from a chaplain in Iraq paraphrased a passage from the Bible to equate the Good Book to the plight of the soldier and the help that OTS provided. He referenced Matthew 25:35 by saying, "When we were hungry, you gave us something to eat, and when we were thirsty, you gave us something to drink. We were strangers to you, yet you became my friend." He concluded with the thought that what we had given his people would bless them in ways we might never know. This was a beautiful sentiment and seemed to apply to our mission perfectly.

An unexpected call from the Danvers Diversity Council brought to us a very pleasant surprise. The council had selected OTS as their recipient of the Martin Luther King Diversity Award for the year, due to our involvement with the soldiers, regardless of race, color, religion, or ethnic background. This unexpected announcement culminated with a 250-attendee dinner at the Danversport Yacht Club one beautiful spring evening. On that occasion, it was announced that Christine and Dick Moody were selected as the Danvers Citizens of the Year, which was truly unexpected but very much appreciated.

OTS and the National Guard

One day, I received a call from a representative from the National Guard. He let me know that some of his guardsmen who had been called up to active duty had received some care packages from our organization and had informed him about it. He was very impressed with our mission and asked for more information. Over the next few weeks, he noticed that I asked for donations from my workplace at Metcalf & Eddy in Wakefield and received quite a large number of contributions. As a result, he had recommended our company be recognized by the National Guard. A short time later, he called to inform me that Metcalf & Eddy was the recipient of a beautiful certificate from the National Guard for remembering our soldiers. This led to some recognition for Operation Troop Support, and we invited him and his staff to a couple of our packing events.

The Guard units played an active role in the OTS annual dinner, serving as our color guard and helping us find ways to help the Guard's children with recreational events. We sponsored the summer family picnic and the Guard's Christmas party for several years. In turn, we received donations and recognition for our work with the troops.

One year, the National Guard contacted me and announced that OTS had won their annual award for helping the Guard and its families. As a result, they invited Christine and me to the Massachusetts Military Reservation on Cape Cod to tour the facilities and get exposure on some of the equipment. This was a wonderful experience, resulting in a ride on a Blackhawk helicopter and a session on shooting the weapons used by the soldiers.

Christine firing weapons at the Mass. Military Reservation

One rather humorous incident occurred during the visit to the Cape. When I had returned from Iraq, I related my experience on the Blackhawk and the combat descent. On the chopper, I was sitting on the edge on the side in an open door, with nothing but a safety belt holding me in. I told Christine that the approach to the landing field was a very scary time for me because of the quick, erratic turns. As I've just mentioned, at the Massachusetts Military Reservation, we were treated to a ride in a Blackhawk. Christine was in the middle seat; the doors were closed. We were flying at about five thousand feet, straight and level, over the Cape Cod Canal. She looked at me and said, "You wimp; this isn't scary a bit." Sometimes, it's best to leave well enough alone.

Predeployment Seminars

In our dealings with the National Guard, we had the opportunity to do more than just send care packages. We were invited to attend the predeployment seminars that the military ran for the soldiers and their families a couple of weeks before the deployment occurred. This was a wonderful idea because it prepared the soldier for his or her assignment and presented a whole array of useful information that the families could use while their loved ones were away. During these seminars, which the soldier and family attended together, topics such as health care and financial, educational, and legal advice are given, along with telephone numbers of representatives to call while the soldier is away.

In addition to the predeployment briefings, the Department of Defense and the Veterans Administration banded together to run the program to provide relevant information to the families, while their loved ones transitioned back into society following their time away. These postdeployment seminars were just as important as the earlier meetings because they dealt specifically with the issue of readjustment.

During the time away, soldiers experienced things they most likely never had gone through before. These often-horrific encounters could have a devastating impact on the mind, causing reactions of fear, rage, lack of sleep, sudden mood swings, deep depression, and a lot of other mental and physical reactions. These attitudes were mostly reactive in nature and beyond the control of the individual, unless he or she got help. The family had to know how to cope with this change in their loved one.

On the other side, the family had just gone through a long period of being on their own. Perhaps the spouse had taken over the payment of the monthly bills, rearranged part of the house, and become more independent with his or her life and the lives of their children. Some of the responsibilities that previously were handled by the deployed soldier now had been assumed by the spouse at home. Conflicts between ways of dealing with circumstances could lead to tension in the house. Put all these changes together, and one could easily see the need for counseling or therapy after the deployment was over. The postdeployment meetings were every bit as critical as the earlier seminars, but unfortunately, many of the families overlooked this very important opportunity.

OTS went to most of the predeployment seminars and set up a table to specifically speak to the families regarding family support, participation in care page and Christmas programs, social events among other families experiencing the same trauma, and our phone number, just in case the family member wanted to talk. The program was very successful, and we made a lot of contacts at this event.

Below are some pictures taken at one of the predeployment seminars:

OTS volunteers speaking with families at the Yellow Ribbon Seminar

OTS and the NMFA

We have created many memories over the past years, but a definite highlight came with our trip to Washington, DC, as a result of an invitation from the National Military Family Association (NMFA), a national organization that is noted for supporting and enhancing the quality of life for every military family. They have been the go-to source for administration officials, members of Congress, and other key decision-makers when they want to understand the issues facing the military family. The NMFA is one of the most influential advocacy groups in the country, and Christine and I were especially proud when they asked us to join their advisory board on the recommendation of Mrs. Joanne Patton, an existing board member. The group has ties to organizations across the country, and they sponsor events, legislation, and scholarships for military spouses and their children. One of their most noteworthy programs is the Operation Purple summer camps for the children of military families. These camps are run every summer at no cost to the family and are available to every military child.

The NMFA established a national award called the Very Important Patriot Award, bestowed on certain people or groups who went above and beyond the call of duty to show their patriotism in ways that would help Americans in uniform or their families. We were selected, along with four other recipients from across the country, to receive this prestigious award. As such, we were called to Washington to receive the honor.

The first evening after we arrived in the nation's capital, we had dinner at General Casey's home. General Casey was the commanding general of the US troops in the Middle East, and although he was unable to be with us that night, Mrs. Casey treated us as if we were old family friends. The next morning, we were taken on a tour of the Pentagon and the Capitol Building, where we met the Massachusetts senatorial staff. That evening, the grand dinner was sponsored by Coca-Cola and Kellogg's cereals, and it was there that we received the Patriot Award for the year. Following the dinner, the photographer took our pictures. A few months later, we found ourselves on the box of Kellogg's Frosted Flakes. This was a surprise and drew a lot of attention on the home front.

VIP Award winners including Dick and Christine Moody

OTS Day at the Farm

Another highlight of our summer was an event hosted by Mrs. Joanne Patton, which we dubbed OTS Day at the Farm. The Green Meadows Farm was started by Major General George Patton upon his retirement from the army in 1980. The general had passed away, but his widow, Joanne, had kept the business going and had decided to host an annual OTS Day at the Farm. Each year, the volunteers were treated to a wonderful cookout, backed up by some talented musicians, whom she brought on for our listening enjoyment—from Dixieland bands, to jazz combos, to the big band groups, to the singing marine sergeant Dan Clark. During the afternoon, we had delightful conversations, rode around the trails on a hayride, and walked about the fields, which were full of the crops for the year. It was a beautiful day and gave us the opportunity to relax and socialize with our group on a sunny summer afternoon.

During our OTS Day at the Farm in 2010, a very special thing happened. The day was sunny and warm, and Joanne Patton was her usual charming, engaging self. All of our volunteers were having a great time, and when the music of the patriotic band finished up a great rendition of "When Johnny Comes Marching Home Again," Joanne asked for everyone's attention. Then she said she had something to show us and asked that we all follow her. To best describe it, I've included an article from the local paper on the events of that afternoon:

After a spirited day at the annual Operation Troop Support Day at Patton Farm, Mrs. Joanne Patton told the crowd she had a special surprise for them and asked if they would follow her on a short walk.

Mrs. Patton excitedly marched ahead leading the crowd to music by the "Uncle Sam's Patriotic Band." The guests marched past the pigs and chickens that scattered as the trombone belted out "As the Saints Come Marching In." They marched down a path to an open field where Mrs. Patton stopped next to a large boulder that was obscured in front by a covering.

Mrs. Patton explained that she wanted to continue a tradition her husband, Major General George S. Patton, had started after he returned home from serving 34 years in the military. When Patton came home to Massachusetts to begin his farm career, he started a tradition to honor those fallen heroes that had served with him in Vietnam and Korea. Patton would name a field in tribute to them.

"It was important to him," Joanne Patton said. "My husband said he couldn't bring them back, but he would never forget them or let the world forget either." As the covering was removed from the boulder by head farmer Andrew Rodgers, a newly created plaque, dedicated to Operation Troop Support shone in the sun. Patton named the field in honor of the organization that sends packages to the troops in harm's way overseas. Turning to the open field, Patton said this would be a field of hope. A field of promise. "I promise that this will be a forever field. We will always remember those who have served and their families".

Dick Moody, along with his wife Christine, were visibly moved. "We work hard but don't ever expect anything in return," said Moody. "So something like this is so heartfelt and was really unexpected. This will stay in our hearts forever."

Dedication of the OTS Field

OTS Sign at the Patton Field

Because the name of Operation Troop Support was becoming associated with the soldiers fighting overseas, we were asked to make a presence at many different events. In our discussions with the American Red Cross, we knew that blood was needed, so we hosted a blood drive at the local chapter, which was well received by many people, some of whom were our OTS volunteers. We attended the National

Day of Prayer at one of the churches on the North Shore, and we were asked to speak on the welfare of the troops and how we were bringing comfort to them.

One evening, we received a call from a representative of the West Point Society of New England (WPSNE), who had decided to run a fundraising raffle at its annual dinner and to donate the proceeds from the raffle to us. We were thrilled to be honored this way, and on the night of the dinner, which we were asked to attend, we met some wonderful soldiers of the Long Gray Line, the alumni of West Point. In the large army population in the convention hall, I decided to keep my air force background tucked quietly away while in their presence. It was a great evening, and OTS was presented with a sizable donation.

As the holidays approached, the letters from the troops continued to arrive. One such letter was passed to us in December by the aunt of a soldier. She read a message from her nephew in Iraq who had received holiday gifts from OTS. In this message, he asked his aunt to please thank our organization for him because the gifts had unexpectedly arrived and had brightened up his unit's Christmas.

When feedback such as this came in, it was wonderful because it showed us that we were still doing the right thing for our heroes in a faraway land.

Over the next few weeks, we received beautiful certificates of appreciation from the combat units in country, along with photos of the men and women holding up the items that we had sent to them. Some of the units sent us American flags that they had flown over the enemy territory. These meant so much to us, as I'm sure the packages did to them.

TRAGEDY STRIKES

As Operation Troop Support was gaining momentum and more volunteers came to our side, one mother in particular, Carol Slavin, became a huge help to us and assisted at every event. Carol became an integral part of the decision-making team, and Christine and I counted on her input whenever a new event was planned. Carol's son TJ was in Iraq, and this bond brought us close together, while showing others why the Family Support Group was so important.

As we learned, the common thread that binds families and individuals together during a deployment can never be felt completely until the loved one comes home, and even after that, a deep-felt kinship remains by those who went through the ordeal. Most of us are very fortunate that our family member completes his or her tour of duty and returns to us safely.

As we know, however, things don't always go as planned or anticipated, and this was borne out one morning when we received a call that TJ Slavin had been severely injured by an IED (improvised explosive device) in Iraq. He was being rushed home to the States, where the staff at Walter Reed Army Medical Center in Washington, DC, was set to operate. Carol, of course, was already on her way down when I received the word that her son had taken a very serious hit.

He had suffered a broken left leg, a crushed lumbar spine, and internal injuries, along with cuts and abrasions. The first leg surgery was performed at the Tenth Combat Support Hospital in Baghdad, and then he was flown directly to Washington, DC, where he was admitted to Walter Reed for a second surgery.

I passed the word to the other volunteers, and after the shock of the incident began to settle, we all prayed that he would be spared any permanent injuries.

Christine comforting Carol
after hearing of her son's injuries

TJ's injury occurred in the summer, and in October, I traveled to Walter Reed to see how he was progressing. While Christine and I knew Carol well, I had never personally met TJ and didn't know what he looked like. As I stood outside his door at the Mologne House, the Walter Reed convalescent facility, I envisioned going into a room with a patient tied up with traction ropes and head bandages. Then the door opened, and I was looking at a good-looking young man in sneakers, wearing a Boston Red Sox sweatsuit and a Red Sox ball cap on backwards.

Looking beyond the person standing in front of me and scanning the room for a wounded soldier, I asked if TJ were here. The greeter answered that he was, and again I looked around the room to find the subject of my search. When I asked a second time if I could see him, the fellow at the door quietly stated that he was TJ.

I thought he was kidding. Was this some type of bad joke? TJ had just come through a terrible ordeal, broken all kinds of bones, and experienced an exceedingly awful trauma. This baseball player couldn't possibly be him.

Well, he finally convinced me he was, in fact, TJ Slavin, Iraqi veteran, recuperating patient, who had undergone multiple surgeries and was on the mend. In three months, the military doctors at Walter Reed had put my friend's son back together. I was astounded, and from that day forward, I became a good friend of a very tough army soldier.

It is very difficult for a person who has never experienced the turbulent times or excruciating worry that accompanies a military deployment to understand and appreciate the emotional impact it has on a family. In addition, it is nearly impossible to feel the effects of a military deployment, especially in a wartime environment, on the soldier experiencing it. One of the underlying points that the OTS Family Support Group stressed was the need to prepare yourself for what the future may hold. This is a concern that is often overlooked.

Christine and I were very fortunate to attend TJ Slavin's wedding a few months after the terrible event, and to many, he was the happy-go-lucky guy with a beautiful wife who was set to embark on a wonderful life together. Only a few people knew the ordeal that he and his family had gone through prior to getting to that glorious day.

Almost on a daily basis, we received messages from the troops, expressing their joy at our commitment to them. These messages meant so much to our group when they used such phrases as, "We are honored to be in the thoughts of great Americans such as yourselves," or "What a blessing it is to have you to remember all the troops that pass through here. Our men and women are all so appreciative of the items that you have so graciously provided them."

The war came home to us in a very personal way in February 2007. We had been sending packages to a Rob Svoboda, a soldier in Iraq, for months. He called us one day to tell us to stop sending packages, as he was coming home because his brother Brad, who was in the army, had been killed in the line of duty. This was a shock to me, and I tried to find out more information on this Danvers soldier.

Brad Svoboda was a staff sergeant in the Ninety-Fourth Military Police Company out of Manchester, New Hampshire. He had spent his time in Iraq but had returned from combat a few weeks earlier. He had volunteered for a short-term humanitarian mission in Panama to seek out possible landing zones for medevac helicopters.

The mountain roads were very dangerous, and another vehicle had a head-on crash with his HMMWV, killing both Brad and the occupant of the other vehicle. The OTS team met with his heartbroken mother and raised money to help her get through the trauma. This was a personal hometown tragedy that put our minds and hearts on the realism of the dangers of the war.

SSgt Brad Svoboda

Dealing with the troops who are stationed in a war zone gives us the opportunity to hear some very realistic feedback, as well as very sad and disturbing stories. The above two examples of the sad stories are only a sampling of the messages that we have received during the war. I shudder every day that there may be more notifications around the corner. Some soldiers who were close to me have perished, and I only hope that they are in a far better place today.

Even as we grappled with the sad turn of events, the exposure and recognition we received during the past year encouraged us to experiment with other ways to support our troops. We expanded our outreach program by visiting schools, churches, civic groups, outside businesses, and health care facilities. We received calls from teachers asking if their students could make cards for the soldiers for Valentine's Day, Easter, or Memorial Day, to which we said absolutely. On many occasions, I would visit the school to encourage their participation.

The Impact of a Letter

I received a call from the middle school in town, asking if I would be their guest speaker on Memorial Day. I love to speak passionately on OTS, but I was looking for some words that would be unique for Memorial Day. About a week before my speech, I received a letter from a soldier in Iraq who had been terribly despondent. He had been in country for months, and during that time, he had not received any mail, emails, texts, postcards, or packages from home. No one remembered that he was fighting in Iraq, and he felt all alone. He told me in his letter that he believed no one would miss him if he took his own life.

That same day, when he was at his lowest point, the mail came, and he was shocked when his name was called to pick up a letter. He opened the envelope and read a handwritten message:

We are so proud of you for defending America and taking the risk to fight for our country. Be safe and return soon to America. We love you and think you're great.

The letter was signed, "A student at Holten Richmond Middle School, Danvers, MA."

In his letter to me, he said that reading that note gave him such a boost to feel that someone actually cared about him, and it changed his attitude that morning. How had this happened?

Well, we had included several handwritten cards and sent them to his unit about a week earlier. When we did this, we always left the envelopes blank, so our contacts could write the names of those men and women who had not been getting much mail. Someone had put his name on the envelope, and it made that note personal to him.

I now saw that I had the makings of a good speech for the Holten Richmond Middle School classes on the Memorial Day visit. When the day came, I told the students and faculty the story of the soldier, and after I finished, I looked around the auditorium and pointed to several students. I asked, "Was it your letter? Was it your letter? How about you? Was it your letter? Don't *ever* underestimate the power that one letter can have over the emotions or life of another person. That note may have saved that poor soldier's life that day. Please remember our family members who are in battle."

When I finished speaking, I walked off the stage, and nearly one hundred students came up to me, asking for the address of a soldier so they could write to him or her. That is what it's all about—taking care of our troops. That is what OTS is all about.

The Guard Member Who Lost Everything

One day, we received a call from the local National Guard unit that one of their soldiers was in trouble. We had been in the middle of a terrible nor'easter, and one young lady, who lived alone on the coast with her cat, had moved inland the day before to spend the night with a friend during the terrible weather conditions.

The next morning, she went to check on her shoreline house, and it had been completely destroyed by the storm. She was left homeless, with no furniture, clothing, bed linens, towels, food, utensils, or personal belongings. Everything was gone. The unit asked if OTS could help her in any way. We sent out an urgent request to everyone on our email list, explaining the situation, and within a few hours, donations were dropped off at our home. We received food, clothing, gift cards to stores, lots of cat food, and other items that were perfect, considering the size of the tragedy. I visited her unit at Camp Curtis Guild in Wakefield, Massachusetts, and met with her. She was so thankful for the donations and wanted everyone to know that we had given her some lifesaving help. She might not have been deployed, but she was a soldier in need of help, and OTS was able to take care of the situation.

OTS Down Range

Over the first few months of OTS, Christine and I made many new friends, and we became a family with a common purpose. We looked forward to seeing everyone on a regular basis, and we enjoyed the feedback from the families as they relayed to us the messages from their loved ones in the combat zone. In the early years, our packages went to Iraq, Afghanistan, Kuwait, UAE, and Qatar. As we expanded, however, and more deployments came, the area expanded. The areas that we were made aware of included the above locations, plus Djibouti, Saudi Arabia, Nigeria, Poland, Romania, Bulgaria, and the Bahamas. This last one was made evident to me when we received a thank-you note one day from a sergeant in the Bahamas. It seemed that his small detachment was a member of a larger battalion in Iraq, and for some reason, they were sent to the Bahamas on orders. I responded to the sergeant that if I had known they were down there, I might have delivered the package myself!

At first, we sent our care packages to soldiers by name, resulting from requests from family and friends, but as our packages reached more people, and they read the Care Package Request form that was included in every box, we started getting more and more requests.

Letters from the United Services Organization (USO) and the American Red Cross started coming in, with personal notes asking for our help. They specifically asked if we would send packages to them, as troops were always coming through their area, and they wanted to have toiletries, games, books, and snacks ready to give out when a battle-weary soldier stepped through the doorway.

The next major request came from the chaplains of the various groups. The chaplains were in the field with the soldiers, and they saw some pretty awful things. They would write to us and tell us of the need they had for items to share with the soldier when he or she came in to talk to them and ask for advice or guidance. At those times, having something to comfort them was a huge help. The rest of the packages went to the troops directly, and we would receive feedback on a continuous basis, thanking us for sending them items that gave them a morale boost.

Periodically, we would receive a photo of one of the soldiers holding a care package in his or her hand, and this meant a lot to us, considering we often wondered if they were enjoying our packages. One day, we received a photo of three young female soldiers, holding up a box of cereal that we had sent. They also held a sign that read, "Thank you for breakfast." That little phrase meant a lot to us—we had connected with those soldiers.

We received a note from a major in the British army. He thanked us and told us our gift was very special to him, as no similar group in England had done anything like this. He decided to bring it back to England at Christmas and open it on Christmas morning while his family was beside him. He said that it meant so much to him, knowing that his comrades in arms had reached out to take care of him while he was on remote duty.

A very surprising moment came when we received a letter from a general in the Mongolian army. I hadn't even known that Mongolia had an army, but I know he was appreciative of our kindness. He happened to be located with some of our troops, who gave him a few of the items in our care package. We were moved by his letter but were even more taken by the fact that our soldiers were able to share our gifts with some of their comrades, even those from other countries.

We received all sorts of thank-you notes, cards, and letters from the troops throughout the years, and they have been especially generous in their gifts back to us. We have received a US flag that was flown in the Blackhawk helicopter during a mission, plus a challenge coin from the commander of the squadron. We received a monument of a unit cut out of stone, and a guidon from a squadron of Reserve soldiers who were deployed to the war zone. Numerous certificates of appreciation were forwarded to us, and we were highlighted in one of the squadrons' newsletters.

One night in Boston, there was a knock on our car door as we were leaving an event—it was a soldier who had recognized the OTS logo on our vehicle and wanted to personally thank us for the gifts we had sent him while he was deployed. He had recently returned, and he told us our care packages were lifesavers over there. Hearing that really made our evening complete.

I love to tell the story of the night when a flight attendant spoke at our Family Support Group. Her brother was a captain in the military and was stationed in Iraq at a small FOB (forward operating base). It was Christmas, and the unit had erected a small artificial Christmas tree, hoping to bring some Christmas spirit to the men and women. On Christmas morning, the tree had no gifts under it, so the crew put all of their Christmas cards under the artificial branches to decorate the area. At about 10:00 a.m., the mail truck pulled up and delivered over one hundred Christmas gifts from Operation Troop Support. The captain was so excited that they could celebrate Christmas, and he asked his sister to find us and say thank you from the soldiers because it had meant so much to them. These are the stories that make it all worth the long hours we put in.

FROM OUR HOME TO OUR HEROES

We received word from the combat hospital at Balad in Iraq that the soldiers awaiting surgery or who were healing following an operation did not have much to do to keep their mind off their pain. OTS sent boxes of magazines and small handheld games to the hospital, and these were a blessing to the patients, who needed to divert their attention during their hospital stay.

In another instance, we learned that the hospital patients who were scheduled to fly home to Washington, DC, and Walter Reed Army Hospital needed to take their hospital bed sheets with them for the trip to the States. This created a shortage of bed sheets for the hospital. OTS stepped in and sent hundreds of new, clean white bed sheets to the hospital to the delight of our soldiers residing there.

On a daily basis, we received thank-you letters, and this let us know that we were doing something that really mattered. On my trip to Iraq, I saw firsthand what our packages meant to the soldier, and I will always remember the joy of seeing their faces light up when a little bit of home came their way.

ANGELS AMONG US

The events that OTS planned and carried out were excellent in getting our volunteers out of the house and in a group of like-minded family members, where they could talk among each other and get some sort of understanding of their plight. Our events promoted even more donations, and eventually, people realized that our packages required postage fees. The concept of free postage in a war zone applied only to soldiers sending letters back to the States, not for letters and packages traveling from the States to the battlefield. As people realized that OTS was responsible for paying its own postage, they began calculating the cost of sending donated items to their loved ones overseas. OTS was sending 150 boxes every week to soldiers in nearly a dozen countries. At a cost of seventeen dollars per box, one could see that we were spending over $2,500 every week on postage. As this sank in, people who had contacts in the postal system, from the postmaster general on down, vowed to get some type of exemption for OTS because we were sending so many boxes. Unfortunately, nothing ever came of this, but it brought to many peoples' attention the fact that we needed monetary help. Money started coming in the form of grants, gifts, business events, organizational fundraisers, and direct donations.

While the funding was improving, the service we provided to the soldiers, sailors, airmen, and marines continued to take our time. With all the hard work our volunteers did, however, it seemed well worth the effort when we received a note like the following at the end of a hard day:

> Dear Mr. and Mrs. Moody,
>
> As the director of the _____Center, I want to personally thank you for your support and patriotism. Our soldiers are so far from home and their loved ones, and the contents of your packages lift their spirits. But more than that, the mere fact that someone is thinking of them makes us want to thank you from the bottom of our hearts.
>
> Colonel _____
> Kuwait

Our annual dinners tended to open the door to non-OTS people, and this led to outside monetary contributions as well as donations of items. Little by little, we started getting calls from organizations that wanted to do something for the troops, with the proceeds coming to OTS.

Danvers Youth Soccer Tournament

One night, we received a call from Jeff Chambers, a member of the board for the Danvers Youth Soccer League, who informed us that they were having a soccer tournament over the Veterans Day weekend, and they wanted OTS to be the recipient of the proceeds. We were delighted, and the only thing Jeff asked of us was to staff a table at the event, explaining our mission to those who attended. He explained that every Veterans Day, a youth soccer tournament was held, with forty to fifty teams participating from across the state. Entry fees were required, referees were hired, food was brought in, equipment such as nets, goalposts, and balls were rented, and shirts commemorating the event were stitched.

We set up some tables to collect donations from the soccer teams, and we had Christmas cards available for the soccer players to sign to a soldier between the games. The Soccer Board authorized the tournament for OTS; then they contacted the organizations involved to see if they could agree to a reduced price that would allow the majority of the proceeds to go to OTS. The feedback that OTS received was that the $400 entry fee per team would come to us, plus the proceeds from the sale of food and shirts. The equipment company donated the nets and goals free of charge, and the referees donated their time. Everyone was willing to give up a Saturday and Sunday in November for the troops.

Over the years, this Soccer for the Soldiers Tournament has become one of the largest events of the fall season in Danvers. Each year, more and more towns have brought donations to the table on the day of the games, and we have received countless monetary donations as well. One town brought in eighteen regular-size Christmas stockings, decorated for the troops, and each was filled with all sorts of gifts for the soldiers. We sent these treasures to the soldiers just as they were, since the young players had taken the time to put them together.

As it turned out, over forty-five towns across the state signed up for the event, so we had the opportunity to showcase the soldiers' needs to a lot of people. This was the initial event that would become an annual highlight for the next fifteen years. As the founders of OTS, Christine and I believe that this is one of the greatest outpourings of community patriotism that we have seen—everyone working and sacrificing for the good of the American soldier. Wow!

The beauty of the tournament was that everybody did their part to ensure our military men and women were cared for. Over the years, this tournament has brought in over $100,000 to OTS, as well as a large cash donation from the parents, thousands of cards and letters written by the young players between their games, and a whole lot of goodwill for all. People went home knowing they had done something good for our soldiers. The Board of Directors of the Danvers Youth Soccer League deserves high marks for demonstrating how America can reach out and help their heroes.

Players compete at the Youth Soccer tournament

Players write cards to the troops

Axcelis Technologies, Inc. Golf Tournament

At about the same time as the soccer tournament, Axcelis Technologies, Inc., of Beverly, Massachusetts, contacted us to say they would like to host a golf tournament and give the proceeds to OTS. Vice President Chris George was in charge of the day-to-day planning and coordinated with us on a continuous basis in the planning and running of the event. With the help of Jill Parsons, Annmarie Stevens, and Jan Pretty, the day went off beautifully.

The tournament was held at the Haverhill Country Club, a beautiful eighteen-hole golf course with large function rooms for special occasions. Chris and his committee executed the perfect event and set out some beautiful raffles, with new clubs, balls, shirts, gift cards, and other quality items offered as raffle prizes.

The club put on a great buffet luncheon, and they asked OTS to set up a table to explain our mission and give the players a few words on our success. We explained what we did and how our packages helped the soldiers get through their tours of duty. The day went off perfectly, and they presented us with a check for several thousand dollars for our postage.

As with the soccer event, Axcelis has continued to run this tournament every year, and this past year, their donation was over $18,000, bringing the total of donations over the years to over $100,000 as well. What an incredible act of kindness to say to our soldiers, "We care!"

One of the wonderful side benefits of the golf tournament is that many of the companies with which Axcelis works who sponsored the event have become supporters of OTS on their own over the past few years, and this has been an invaluable source of income for our organization.

Carts ready for the big Show   The day on the fairway

Blues for the Troops

One afternoon, I ran into a friend, Leo Rizzotti, and he wanted to know if he could help us with an event he had been thinking of. Leo was a great musician, and he led a blues band that had been started by his father, Lee Hawkins. Leo believed he could get a few more groups together and put on a musical show, with the proceeds going to OTS. We discussed the idea, and we said we would come watch him perform the next weekend at the Polish American Club in Danvers.

We loved what we heard at the event. Leo had some contacts, and he organized a musical show for a Sunday afternoon a few weeks later. He asked his friend Dave Papa to help organize the show, and Dave became a very dear friend. Dave was a gifted musician, as was Leo, but his role in the upcoming show was to put together a raffle table. What a great job he did. His raffle prizes included guitars and music memorabilia, plus a host of other beautiful items that would sell a lot of raffle tickets.

It was decided that the cost to the public would be ten dollars at the door, and that money would go to OTS. Inside the hall, OTS would set up a table, and we could sell any products of our own, which primarily consisted of shirts or hats that we had printed up with our logo on them. Leo brought in four or five blues bands who agreed to play for no charge for the day. The music was superb, and the crowd was huge. Leo christened the event Blues for the Troops, and that name stayed with the event for years. Every year, we would have a blues event, and Leo and Dave would preside over the great concert. Other groups tried to get a spot in the lineup, and the doors continued to be loaded with concert-goers every year. OTS reaped the rewards of an excellent afternoon of outstanding blues music, and we owe it to Leo Rizzotti and Dave Papa, two outstanding musicians with a vision to help the troops.

The crowd enjoying the
Blues for the Troops

Leo Rizzotti, the organizer of
the Blues performing on stage

Bike Runs

Soccer, golf, and music had worked out well, but then we received a call from a motorcycle group, who asked if we would be interested in their group sponsoring a bike run. We said we would love it, and they planned it for a day that, fortunately, turned out to be absolutely beautiful. On that morning, OTS was in the midst of over one hundred men and women who did what they loved for a cause that they believed in. What a great combination.

Over the years, certain biker clubs have continued to help OTS. Our first ride was with the Enforcers of Somerville, Massachusetts. These riders were mostly law enforcement officers, and they ran a great event for us. Shortly after that run, a local group known as the Falcon Riders from the Danvers area put together a run, which we combined with a cookout. This was a fun day, and it exposed the riders to our OTS team, which was very beneficial for them as well as for our group.

After the Somerville run, we got involved with the Legion Riders of various American Legion posts. For the most part, the American Legion Post 127 from Middleton, Massachusetts, was the base for the runs for OTS. We would start with a patriotic ceremony in the morning, followed by a great cookout and entertainment following the ride.

All the riders were fantastic, but three, in particular, were at every event and went the extra mile for us—Doug Tinsley, Sam Demao, and Curt Alboth. Under Doug's leadership, the Legion Riders became an integral part of the OTS mission. They worked with other Legion posts and arranged runs over the years. Their role consisted of planning the routes, coordinating with the home posts, notifying the towns and their police departments that we would be coming through their streets, and working as the liaison with OTS to ensure the day went off without a hitch. We owe a great deal of thanks to these three individuals and will stay friends with them for years to come.

While the Legion Riders did a great job for OTS, another group of American Legion individuals made major contributions to the mission. These were the American Legion auxiliaries in the various posts. Our closest allies were the members of Post 127 Auxiliary, with special focus on Ms. Bonnie Amore and Ms. Joan Flynn. On the days of the bike runs, we had raffles and a bake sale to top off the festivities. These two individuals, along with so many other members, always helped us out with monetary donations, food for the runs, raffle items for our raffle, food for our bake sale, and participation in any number of duties on the day of the run. Of particular note, we were given great attention by the legion hall managers, Mark and Mike Pelletier, as well as Ms. Pam Monroe, the Legion Riders' president, who took care of the details on so many of the rides for us. OTS is extremely grateful to the post and the auxiliary for their hard work, dedication, and patriotism.

On the days of the run, our OTS volunteers usually staffed the registration table and had every biker sign in, which included signing a limitation of liability that waived any responsibility or liability of OTS or the post, in the event a biker got hurt or damaged anyone's property. We would also set up an OTS table to provide pamphlets and other handouts for the attendees, as well as selling the OTS shirts and hats. When the run started, I would usually drive the OTS truck with the flags and OTS logo at the beginning of the lineup. This would be good advertising to explain why the run was taking place.

As the years went on, more and more motorcycle clubs contacted me and asked if they could do a bike run for the troops. As mentioned earlier, OTS loved this, because the biker community is super patriotic, and it was inspiring being around them when they had a run. Bikers from Middleton, Danvers, Haverhill, Saugus, Manchester, and Boston have participated, and nearly all of them ended their runs with a cookout or pig roast and raffles. These runs generated a lot of monetary support for the troops, and they brought to us names of soldiers who were currently stationed or about to go to the desert.

The Bikers arriving for the Bike run.

OTS Special Memories

These last twenty years have been filled with so many great things. Christine and I have met some wonderful people, and we have communicated with very special men and women who have put their lives on the line for the country they love. If we could, we would thank everyone who has crossed our paths, but we cannot do that within the confines of this book. There have a been few special situations, however, that have stayed with us through the years, and we'd like to share them with you here.

Working with the Girl Scouts

The old saying goes, "When the going gets tough, the tough eat cookies." This is proven every year at Girl Scout cookie time. The Girl Scouts of Eastern Massachusetts contacted OTS several years ago and asked if we could take some cookies and send them to the troops. We were happy to oblige, and each year, I pull the OTS trailer to Hanscom Air Force Base, where the OTS volunteers pack hundreds of cases of cookies of all varieties. We send them out to the far corners of the earth, where the soldiers get total enjoyment out of the treats. We have been working with the Girl Scouts for years, and it is a wonderful experience to work on this effort with them.

As the Girl Scouts sell their cookies to the public, they have signs or usually ask if the buyer is willing to purchase an extra box for the troops. Most people do, and the Girl Scouts put aside these boxes, which total several hundred cases by the time they are ready to send them to the troops. At that time of year, they call four or five organizations who have ties with the troops and ask them to pick up the cookies on a certain day. Since the handout location is Hanscom Air Force Base in Bedford, we need to coordinate with the volunteers and send their contact information to the base ahead of time. This is to give the base the opportunity to ensure that everyone entering the facility is cleared to do so. Then, on the day of the pickup, each vehicle is checked upon arrival at the base. In addition, everyone entering must have adequate identification so that the military guards can check their information against the earlier list they have received. Provided everything is in order, then we are cleared to enter the base.

The cookies sit on loaded pallets, and the military personnel stand by to help the OTS volunteers load the cases into our vehicle. Then we close up the trailer and come back to Danvers. As one would expect, the next few shipments to the troops are heavily filled with cookies, and the troops love them.

Working with the Girl Scouts has been so rewarding. The organization is doing an excellent job of promoting their program, while doing something that the soldiers love. Girl Scout cookies are a tradition that reminds the soldier of home, and this alone is worth the effort to sell, collect, and send these gems to the troops. Oh, they taste great too.

Military helps OTS with their cookies

From palette to trailer to soldier

Saving Johnny

I love the story of Johnny. I received a telephone call one afternoon from the veterinarian at Hanscom Air Force Base, who asked for my help. She had a military German shepherd dog named Johnny that recently had returned from Iraq. Overseas, Johnny had been a bomb-sniffing dog and had been in country for about a year. No issues occurred during his deployment, but during the second week back at Hanscom, he slipped on a wet platform and slid off the staging, breaking his legs.

The military considered Johnny an asset, much like a gun or a tank. Other assets could be fixed, using money that was appropriated for repairing the asset. No such money had been allotted to "fix"

Johnny, and therefore, the decision was made to put him down. A tearful veterinarian asked us for help. She had inquired about the cost of the surgery to repair the broken bones, and Tufts Veterinary Hospital seemed to have the best price at $2,700. I told her we would try to help and said we drive down to Hanscom to see the poor animal.

The next day, I visited Johnny at the base; he was lying on his side, unable to stand. He looked at me and his tail very slowly wagged, and I knew we had to help him. After I returned home, I sent out an email to everyone on my email list, explaining the situation and asking for a donation, no matter how small, to raise the money for the surgery. Within a few hours, I had online donations or pledges to mail-in contributions that would cover the cost for the Tufts estimate, which had already been reduced, given the circumstances. The surgery was scheduled for a few days out, and on that day, the doctors went to work on Johnny. A few days later, the Hanscom vet called me and joyfully reported that Johnny had come through the surgery and was on the road to recovery.

Over the next few months, we kept in contact with the base, and on a second visit, I found Johnny standing, walking, and even running like a cured patient. I was delighted at the sight and invited him and his trainer to come, as a surprise guest, to our upcoming OTS dinner. On that night, when I announced a very special guest, the doors opened, and Johnny was led in, amid the cheering and clapping of the attendees. Just like in the movies, he came up to me and stood on his hind legs, resting his front paws on my shoulders, as if to say, "See? I'm all better."

His trainer David said they both were leaving the military, after *a long and dedicated* career. They settled on a small farm up in Maine, where Johnny can live out his remaining carefree days.

Johnny, awaiting surgery on his legs

Johnny rests after the operation

World War II Hangar Dance

When a World War II hangar dance is suggested, the initial reaction is often one of delight, nostalgia, and patriotism. Such was the case when the local Civil Air Patrol announced they were sponsoring the event, and they asked if OTS could be a part of the evening.

The event was to be held at one of the hangars at Beverly Airport. In addition to musicians playing the big band music from the 1940s, they also brought in World War II vintage bomber aircraft—four from North Carolina were flown up for the night. The attendees were treated to a close-up view of the P-47 Mustang fighter, along with the three major bombers: the B17 Flying Fortress, the B25 Mitchell, and the B29 Super Fortress. These aircraft were all chalked on the flight line beside the hangar to give the evening a realistic flair.

The hangar was cleaned out, the night was balmy, the WWII decorations were hung, and people showed up, many in costumes and uniforms of the times. Henry and Judy Levesque arrived, and Judy was dressed as Rosie the Riveter, from the World War II picture printed to encourage female participation in the war effort. ***Next to where Judy was sitting was a picture of her from that same era years ago, wearing her Army uniform.*** Steve Kent showed up in a WWII pilot's uniform, as did several other attendees. Steve and his wife, who are excellent dancers, put on quite a show as they breezed across the hangar floor to the big band music. What a great show!

At a point in the evening, OTS was introduced, and we had the opportunity to tell the group that we were looking for any help they might be willing to give.

This was a great evening, seeing people dressed in the garb of the Second World War, doing the old-time dancing, listening to the big band music, seeing the silhouettes of the vintage aircraft outside the hangar door under the moonlit sky.

Christine and Dick at the Hangar Dance

Dancing into the night

OTS Helps the Red Sox Send Packages

One morning, the Boston Red Sox called me and asked if OTS would do the team a huge favor. It seems that the Red Sox organization had run a donation drive for the troops and didn't know how to send out the care packages that they had put together.

When the call came in, asking for our help, I jumped at the opportunity. I asked our volunteers if anyone would like to go to Fenway Park the following Saturday to pick up about one hundred care packages. They gave me a most definite yes, and the following weekend, we took the trailer into Boston and parked right outside the C gate of the fabled Fenway Park.

Within a few minutes, the gate opened, and about two dozen Red Sox employees came out from behind a huge pile of care packages. We had our introductions, and then everybody brought the boxes to the trailer, where they were neatly packed to the last one. It was a great time working with the world champions to take care of our troops.

After chatting with the Red Sox staff for a few minutes, they asked if we would like to look around and go up in the stands. We said absolutely, and for the next half hour, we walked through the nearly empty stadium, taking pictures and having some of the snacks that the team had sent in.

When we finally said our goodbyes, the staff said they hoped we could do it again next year. Of course, we told them we would look forward to it.

About a week later, we received a sizable check from the Red Sox organization to cover the postage for their packages. This was not part of the deal, but we all agreed it was a very nice gesture on the team's part to do this for us. All in all, this was a nice memory.

Travel to Fenway Park to pick up Red Sox care packages

The Fenway crew helps to load the OTS Trailer

Hadley and Chris's Engagement

We had been planning for a while to have a care-package event, and from all indications, it was going to be very well attended. A couple of weeks prior to the day of the pack, however, we found out that one of our volunteers, Hadley, was getting very eager because her fiancé, Chris, was coming home from deployment about the same time as our pack. Other merchants in town also heard the news, and I received a call from the manager of Lorraine Roy, one of the exclusive women's stores in Danvers. She wanted to do something nice for Hadley; she was planning to give her the opportunity to pick out a beautiful formal dress from her collection, and the store would tailor it for her as well at no charge.

As word got around the town, other merchants came forward, and soon several establishments planned to donate to the cause. The Men's Wearhouse contacted us and said they would donate a sport jacket and slacks for her fiancé; the local florist donated a beautiful arrangement of flowers, which they said would be delivered on the day of the pack; three restaurants gave gift certificates for dinners on a night of their choosing; and a Danvers chauffeur offered his services to drive them in a beautiful limousine to and from a plush hotel for the weekend, all expenses paid.

On the day of the pack, we had set up the hall at the middle school, as with any other packing event. Our crew of volunteers came at the appointed time, and to an observer, everything was as it should have been when the pack commenced. Everyone who was there had received a short briefing on what was about to happen, so everyone was aware of the surprise aspect that afternoon.

Shortly after we started our pack, our lookout said that the couple was pulling up to the building. We had invited Hadley's family to the pack, and when her fiancé, Chris, and she walked into the hall, not suspecting anything, everyone in the hall yelled "Surprise!" to the astonished pair.

We had set up a microphone in the corner of the room and a few of us spoke to the happy couple, expressing our relief that Chris had made it home from his deployment safely and wishing the couple well on their future journey. It was a very happy day for all of us, and it was especially wonderful for Hadley and Chris.

The happy couple: Hadley and Chris

The 9/11 Flag Comes to Danvers

Perhaps one of the most memorable events that Christine and I have experienced during our time with OTS was being visited by the 9/11 flag. This was the same American flag that three firefighters raised above the ruins of the World Trade Center in New York following the terrorist attack on September 11, 2001. The flag was taken down shortly after it was raised and was tucked away for safekeeping. Unfortunately, it was misplaced, and for eight years, no one knew where it was.

It was finally discovered by *someone* who was unaware of its importance. However, sensing it was a very old flag, he contacted the local fire department, who contacted the appropriate offices. Once the flag was verified as the one missing from 9/11, the celebrations began.

The 9/11 Commission decided to take it on a fifty-state tour, where wounded warriors, military veterans, first responders, community service heroes, and 9/11 family members were given a once-in-a-lifetime privilege of restoring our national flag to its original format. This would be done by stitching in American flags from each of the fifty states.

Some of the original Fort McHenry flag threads are sown in it, as are threads from the flag that flew on the USS *Missouri* at the World War II surrender. Even part of the flag that was placed over Abraham Lincoln's coffin after he was assassinated was included.

When the flag came to Massachusetts, it was laid out at St. John's Prep in Danvers, and several OTS members were invited to attend a short ceremony. Then the leaders called some of us up to the flag to sew a stitch into the flag. This was an emotional experience, and the image of Christine sewing the piece is a memory that will stay with me forever. The phrase **on the sign** above the flag said it all: "We are rebuilding America, one stitch at a time."

Christine puts a stitch into the 9/11 Flag

OTS volunteers at the 9/11 ceremony

To Be Continued

March 19, 2003, seems like only yesterday. Quite a bit has happened since that day, when we answered an air force nurse's plea to help her patients. We've sent over one million packages to our men and women deployed to Afghanistan, Iraq, Saudi Arabia, Kuwait, Qatar, United Arab Emirates, Nigeria, Djibouti, Poland, Romania, Korea, Germany, Bahrain, and the Bahamas.

We have received product and monetary donations from across the country. We were asked to join the National Military Family Association, headquartered in Washington, DC. We traveled to Iraq and assessed the needs of our soldiers firsthand. Congress entered us into the Federal Register. Kellogg's put us on a cereal box, and we have received many more accolades throughout the years.

Our most important achievement, however, in the last twenty years has come from the officers and enlisted men and women who left their homes in the United States and chose to put on the uniform of their country and wear it proudly overseas, putting their lives on the line and representing America on the world stage. These men and women would call, email, or write to us, just to say thank you.

As the years go on, it is impossible to forget the looks on the faces of the soldiers as they rush off the plane or bus into the waiting arms of their loved ones, or the families as they prepare for the homecoming, brushing the hair of their young children, who may be meeting Daddy for the first time.

Then it happens—the smiles, the hugs, the tears. We at Operation Troop Support know that being there, witnessing that experience, is worth the twenty years we gave to the mission, and we will never forget that joyous moment in time. God bless our soldiers.

The families wait for the loved one to arrive

Welcome Home!

Operation Troop Support has been in existence for twenty years, but we press on every day. There are still soldiers in harm's way, and there are people who want to help. As long as the good Lord allows OTS to help the soldiers, we will continue to do so because we're not done yet! God bless you all for caring.

Printed in the United States
by Baker & Taylor Publisher Services